How to Make 37% Tax-Free Without the Stock Market

How to Make 37% Tax-Free Without the Stock Market

"Secrets to Real Estate Paper"

Mike Warren
Author/Educator/Investor

New York

How To Make 37%, Tax-Free, Without the Stock Market
Secrets to Real Estate Paper

ISBN 978-1-60037-724-2

Library of Congress Control Number: 2009939062

Morgan James Publishing
1225 Franklin Ave., STE 325
Garden City, NY 11530-1693
Toll Free 800-485-4943
www.MorganJamesPublishing.com

Dedication

This book is dedicated to my lovely wife Tia, without whose unending support, feedback and understanding this book would never have been written. This book is also dedicated to my son Bryce and my daughter Holly, who have given me purpose to look beyond today, and start planning for tomorrow.

Table of Contents

Welcome

I would like to thank you for taking the first step towards financial freedom and for taking time out of your busy schedule to learn new techniques to make solid, secure, and often outstanding returns on your money. This book is designed for individuals who want high returns on their investments without the risk of a volatile stock market.

We all know that you can make money in the stock market. Some investors believe in the buy and hold strategy while others try to time the market. There are seminars that encourage you to trade options or futures and courses that attempt to teach you how to become a day trader. While all of these systems work to some extent, they all have one thing in common:

They all require risk and a lot of work!

The work may be nothing more than doing research on a particular stock or company. Other times the work involves watching the market fluctuations, interest rates, the bond market, contacting your broker, using the internet for research and checking business reports or reading investment newsletters. Even after you do all this research you still do not have a guarantee that you will make a higher return than what you could make from a basic CD or mutual fund. And there is research that shows many investors in the stock market lose money every year.

Everything I discuss has been proven to be successful and can generate you thousands of dollars in profits. You might even want to quit that job where you were helping someone else get rich. Now you have the potential to make a six-figure income. Here is what you will learn in the chapters that follow:

- How to make 37%+ tax-free without the stock market using simple, proven strategies
- How you can profit from paper investments
- How to get started with a small amount of money
- How to plan for your children's future
- How you can make thousands of dollars in profits regardless of your financial condition
- How you can make money from the current recession and coming financial and real estate booms

You can make very good returns in the stock market if you research properly, watch the market diligently, have enough money to invest and have a little bit of luck. If you were asked what rate of return you were going to make at the end of the year you knew with almost 100% certainty, would you have the answer? Do you want to put your money in the market where anything can happen, or would you rather have an investment vehicle that can provide you with an average of 37% return each year and every year, perhaps even tax-free?

This book is not about getting rich quick. It is about making choices that are different from the mainstream. By making the right type of investments you can increase your yields while having a high level of security. That does not sound right does it? How can you have high returns unless you have high risk?

You invest where others are not

INTRODUCTION

I have always been a great history buff when it comes to rages-to-riches stories. I like to know how other people pulled themselves up by their bootstraps and made a fortune. I remember going to the library and looking at autobiographies of great people in history. I ran across a book about John. D. Rockefeller. Here was a man that took a very simple idea and created a dynasty out of it. While reading the book I read a quote by Mr. Rockefeller that forever changed my life.

"I always tried to turn every disaster into an opportunity."
John D. Rockefeller

I was at a point in my life where things were not going quite so well. I had just gotten out of the Army and wanted something more out of my life. I didn't have a job but I wanted to travel, have nice cars, a big house, you know the usual stuff. There was only one problem; I did not have any money. While I was sitting there in the public library reading this tremendous book about John D. Rockefeller, I had this revelation. I can turn my life around.

I pulled out some other reference books that wrote about great people in history and I came upon a common theme. The reason over 90% of the American public struggles financially is because they follow the crowd. They assume because everyone else is working or investing in a particular area that it must be a good deal. My goal in this book is to open your mind to a new way to make money that will also put you in the game to win. To win, you need to be focused on what investments or ways of making money are creating the most assets for you.

Another common theme I found was that even though all of these people kept telling Mr. Rockefeller that it could not be done, he did not listen. In fact it made him even more determined to prove everyone wrong. He did just that and laughed all the way to bank while doing it.

I found that whenever I tried something new my friends, family and  associates would tell me that it could not be done. That perhaps it is not legal. That I will lose money. I found that these are all words of the uneducated and the cynical. If someone is not familiar with a type of investment they often try to "put it down" rather than appear like they do not know anything about it. There is a great saying that goes:

Consider Your Source!

I slowly started to learn that life is really a big game. Now don't get me wrong. I still take life seriously and there are some very important issues in everyone's life. I just slowly started to realize that I have a certain role that I am playing in life and it is up to me to gain more skills, knowledge and tools to learn how to play the game to the best of my ability.

Do you remember the first time you ever played a game? I do. I lost. I lost very fast. It was a simple game of checkers, but because

I did not understand the rules I could not play very well and soon lost all of my pieces. As I gained more skill at the game I started to look at strategies that would give me a competitive edge to win the game. I started to read books and play the game a lot. I finally got very good at the game and my confidence grew as a by-product.

To make progress and play to win you first need to step (not leap) out of your comfort zone. The first part of stepping out is to educate yourself. The second step is to analyze the possibilities. The third step is to do it.

But, like John Rockefeller I did not have any money to get started. As a matter of fact I did not even have an idea. I started to read books on investments that would allow me to start small or without any money. I finally ran across this idea of "defaulted paper" as a way to get myself out of the position in life that I was in. I found a unique niche that I could make money where there was virtually no competition and my income was only limited by how well I played the game. And I've used it to provide a very comfortable living for my family and me.

In this book, I'm going to show you exactly how to do the same thing.

As you'll see, there's nothing fancy about this book. It's the street-smart knowledge I've gained over the years... packed into these pages. No glossy paper or pretty pictures here. Just a plain, simple common sense, approach to making great money.

What I'll show you here isn't hypothetical or circumstantial. It's real... the nuts-and-bolts secrets of how I make money in a littler know industry. "Defaulted Paper" also known as "Delinquent

Paper" is a bit misleading, as you'll soon find out. All you will do is simply put into motion the procedures that enable you to make great sums of money.

Quite simply, it's the best way of making money I know.

It is a business that you do not need any money to get started. If you have money, how does making 90% a year on your money sound? More on this later.

I'm proud of what I've done over the past 20 years. I've built a strong business… Over the years I have been in this business I have learned that I really enjoy watching other people become successful and make a lot of money from what I have to teach them. I guarantee that you will learn how to make as much money as you want even if you do not have any money to get started. Just imagine yourself as John Rockefeller when he got started. He did not have anyone to show him what to do and what not to do. Because you are reading this book, you are different. You have already proven that you have the desire to improve your life and your financial condition.

You are about to learn how to make a tremendous amount of money from a resource that is boundless and is virtually untapped. If you have money, even better. I will show you how to get returns on your investments you have only dreamed about.

I'm going to change your life. These techniques that I'm about to teach you are very real and very powerful, and absolutely will change everything about your financial life. It'll help you change it. I know. It changed my life.

CHAPTER ONE

Invest In "Bad" Paper

The term "bad paper" refers specifically to an area called "bad-debts." Now before you jump to any conclusions, let me state that I am going to be very specific on what types of debts to invest in, what to avoid, and how to reduce your risk to almost zero. Bad debts can include such things as:

➢ judgments
➢ judgment liens
➢ tax liens
➢ mechanic liens
➢ defaulted student loans
➢ bank charge-offs
➢ defaulted mortgages

For the purpose of this book I am going to narrow our focus to judgment liens, the most profitable part of the business. As an instructor and investor in the area of bad debts for the past 15 years I have had the privilege of helping people all across the United States and Canada profit from this very lucrative field. I teach multi-day workshops that cover in complete detail how to make money from all types of bad debts. If you are at all like me when I was getting started 20+ years ago, the word JUDGMENT probably doesn't mean a thing. If you already know what they are, then you are ahead of the game. Don't worry, it is very simple. Let me explain…

The first thing anyone needs to do before investing is to understand what it is s/he is investing in. Let me briefly explain what a judgment and a judgment lien is and how they can provide you with above average returns on your investments. A judgment occurs when one person takes another to court and the court awards the winner a judgment against the loser. A judgment lien occurs when the judgment is attached to the debtor's real estate.

The easiest way for me to clarify how the system works is to go back to my beginnings and how I got started in the business.

If you remember from the Introduction, John D. Rockefeller's quote:

> **"I always tried to turn every disaster into an opportunity."**
> **-John D. Rockefeller**

Mr. Rockefeller found ways of turning negatives into positives. I found that assets that people considered to be problems represented huge profits with very little (if any) investment for someone who knew what to do with the paper. Quite literally I found a goldmine in my own back yard and over time I found out that there is plenty of this paper in every city in the country. Most investors ignore bad paper because they do not understand it. Learning how to buy the paper at a huge discount leads to huge returns. In fact, bad paper investors require at least a 30% return on their money per year. That's just the minimum. What if you could double your money each year? Would it make a difference?

But, I am getting way ahead of myself. Let me tell you just some of the many benefits of why bad paper is such a great opportunity and it could cost you thousands of dollars not to learn these techniques.

Let's run through some of the benefits.

Works Anywhere

The paper business has no geographical boundaries. It does not matter where you live now or where you want to live in the future. You can do this work anywhere in the country, whenever the mood strikes you. From the biggest cities to the smallest towns. From Boston to Baton Rouge, Portland to Pasadena. If you're a night  owl, you can do your work at night, leaving your days free for your favorite leisure activities. There is simply so much bad paper available you could never hope to handle it all.

After I got out of the Army and found bad paper I realized I could live and run this business from anywhere I wanted. I chose Colorado, which is where I presently live, because I love the clean mountain air, the skiing and outdoor activities and the slower pace of life. I moved to Colorado. Not because I had to live in Colorado to do the business, but because I wanted to. It was my choice and on my terms. In essence I live in Colorado because I can.

100% Home Based and Employee Free

You can choose to work out of your own home, I don't, but I choose not to because I have a large operation and need employees to handle the large number of deals that are brought to me by students.

You can do the business without having an office downtown or having a bunch of employees with payroll responsibilities, taxes, workers compensation, etc. I mean you can run your paper business out of your home. No more driving to an office building where you work to make someone else rich. There's one bad thing about this business. Weekends lose their importance. It's true. You see when you have so much free time during the week Saturday and Sunday aren't so important. I don't know about you, but that's OK in my book.

You do not need to have a big staff to make money from bad paper. I have had people write me or call me and say how they love the bad paper business because it provides them with immediate cash.

Others who use bad paper as part of their retirement vehicles are excited with the returns they are making in tax-free or tax-deferred retirement plans. Buying paper is only part of the game. And it is a game. But, it is also a business. Which is it you might say? It can be both or neither. It's up to you to have fun with a prosperous new way of life.

Above Average Return on Investment

When you have a little money to invest your rates of return will be better than you could have ever imagined. You Don't Have To Settle For Underachieving Investments such as:

- Low Interest Rate CDs
- Poor Performing Stocks, Bonds or Mutual Funds
- Unsatisfactory Insurance Products

With just a few of the techniques covered in this book you will be able to make consistent double-digit returns on money that you invest. Your money is completely secured by real estate and you are not subject to fluctuating interest rates or the stock market.

 We all know that you can make money in the stock market. Some investors believe in the buy and hold strategy while others try to time the market. There are seminars that encourage you to trade options or futures and courses that attempt to teach you how to become a day trader. The work may be nothing more than doing research on a particular stock or company. Other times the work involves watching the market fluctuations, interest rates, the bond market, contacting your broker, using the internet for research and checking business reports or reading investment newsletters. Even after you do all this research you still do not have a guarantee that you will make a higher return than what you could make from a basic CD or mutual fund. And there is research that shows many investors in the stock market lose money every year.

You can make very good returns in the stock market if you research properly, watch the market diligently, have enough money to invest and have a little bit of luck. If you were asked what rate of return you were going to make at the end of the year you knew with almost 100% certainty, would you have the answer? Do you want to put your money in the market where anything can happen and often does or would you rather have an investment vehicle that can provide you with an average of high double digit and sometimes triple digit returns each year and every year, perhaps even tax-free?

This book is not about getting rich quick. It is about making choices that are different from the mainstream. By making the right type of investments you can increase your yields while having a high level of security. That does not sound right does it? How can you have high returns unless you have high risk?

You invest where others are not.

Virtually no competition.

As you will soon discover, there is a lot of bad paper out in the marketplace but no one knows what to do with it. You see, everyone only wants the good paper. Paper that is receiving a monthly payment every month without any problems. Where the payor (debtor) has perfect credit, a great job and lots of assets. All of the other investors are competing for the same deals. Well guess what, bad paper has very little competition. We (that's you) only want "bad" paper. We can pick and choose the very best of the bad paper to invest in.

Buy Real Estate at Huge Discounts

I guarantee that you will be able to purchase real estate at prices that make buying properties at foreclosures look like you are

paying retail. For anyone that buys foreclosures, buying at 50 – 60 cents on the dollar is fairly commonplace. I am not arguing with this at all. I am simply saying that when you work on the bad paper side of the equation you are able to purchase property for literally pennies on the dollar.

You have a virtually endless supply of paper that you can purchase. There is even more of an opportunity when dealing with bad paper simply because most investors do not know what to do with the paper or how to profit it from the bad paper.

What this means is that since so few people know how to purchase defaulted paper, you are able to get the very best discount on the paper you locate or buy. This equates to a very large return on our investment.

Bad paper = HUGE RETURNS

Tax Free

I'll never forget that day I found out that you could get returns tax-free. Yes that's right, tax-free. The benefits to you and your family are huge. Imagine making your high double-digit returns without having to pay taxes on the gain. I already mentioned that rates of return are in the big double-digit numbers, but imagine making an additional 20% or more on your investments each year. I will explain how you do this, and it will take some explaining on exactly how you do this.

This is a great opportunity if you are looking to make money quickly for retirement or looking to grow your portfolio to outrageous sums over the long term. This is not a loophole but is a time tested IRS approved technique that allows you to quantum grow your investments. I will cover more about tax-free investing in a later chapter.

You know I can go on and on talking about the benefits of this business. But enough is enough, so let's get started into the basics of how and what to do with bad paper.

CHAPTER TWO

Thinking Outside The Box

Before I go into the basics of how to put these deals together I feel it is important to tell you something about myself. I didn't just arrive here with this information in hand. There is a story behind the ideas. So let me tell you how I got started.

Well, let me start by telling you it wasn't easy. You see, as a child I never stayed in any one place for very long. My father was an enlisted man in the United States Army. Being enlisted in the Army meant that we had to move every two years. I learned early on that I should not depend on others for my emotional or financial well-being. Since we moved every two years, I was not able to make long lasting friendships. Not that I couldn't, but simply because it was less painful (emotionally) when we moved if I was not great friends with other kids in my neighborhood. I developed a skill that allowed me to easily develop relationships when we moved to a new area and pick them back up again when I saw my friends.

The Young Entrepreneur

I remember looking around and seeing all of the adults who were not in the military going to work each morning and coming home tired and complaining about their jobs. I remember thinking to myself "boy, I hope I never have to do what they are doing." I was not completely naïve, however. When I was eight years old our family was stationed in Hawaii. I loved to read comic books and eat lots and lots of candy as a kid. I especially loved eating pixie sticks. You know the candy that comes in a straw and is almost all sugar. Well to buy my comics and candy required money and my dad only gave me a little allowance.

So, I started a lawn cutting service. I charged $5 for each lawn. I only cut lawns on the weekend so I was able to cut 4 lawns and make $20. Now that might not seem like a lot, but keep in mind I was only 8 years old. $20 for an 8 year old was a lot of money. Not only was I able to buy comics and candy but I could go to moves and buy other toys. At this age I did not learn very much about saving or investing money. When the money came in, it went right back out.

Cutting lawns required a lot of effort and the truth be told it was not a lot of fun. I thought, gosh, how else can I make money. My first brilliant idea was about to be born.

Dumpster Diving To The Rescue

Have you ever heard that one person's trash is another person's treasure? This is just like John D. Rockefeller's statement about turning a disaster into opportunity. I did not realize it as a child but I was turning other people's disasters into money. I was creating money from an asset that everyone else thought was worthless.

How do I know you might ask? Simple. As a kid living in Hawaii with my father one of my chores was to take out the trash. In the army you don't have a single trashcan that you take out to the curb and a trash truck comes by and picks up your trash. Instead there is a large dumpster that is available for everyone within a neighborhood to place their trash. The special dump truck will come by once a week, lift the dumpster in the air and dump the contents into the back of the dumpster. This actually reminds me of a story my mother loves to tell how as a very small child I climbed into a dumpster just before the trash truck came to pick up the trash. My mother told me how she came out screaming at the trash people not to dump the trash because I was inside the dumpster. I guess that was really my first brush with greatness. Anyway back to my story. When I put our trash bags inside the dumpster I remember looking inside. I am sure you have also looked inside trash areas just out of curiosity to see what other people are throwing away. What I saw were a couple of Archie comic books. Remember I loved comic books and this was an opportunity that was just too good to pass up. I climbed inside and found two Archie comic books. The covers were ripped in half but that didn't matter to me. I had found gold. Each day I would go out to the dumpster to see if any more comic books had been thrown away. Over the span of a couple of months I amassed around 50 different comic books.

In our neighborhood lived a lot of kids. The kids also liked to look at comics. Some of my friends had comics that I wanted very badly but I did not have the money to go out and by the comic. I found my friends were willing to trade their brand new comic for one or two of my used comics. All of a sudden I was negotiating trades on comics. I was getting comics in perfect condition that had great value and trading away comics that someone else wanted that only had limited value to me. I next found myself brokering trades between different friends who could not work out deals on their own. I would trade some of my comics for one or two comics from one friend "A" and negotiate another deal to give one of the comics I got for a couple of comics owned by friend "B". I was multiplying my efforts and I did not even realize it. In the two years my father was stationed in Hawaii I developed a collection of over 1,000 comic books. Without any money. I simply found what others threw away as worthless and sold or traded it to someone who wanted it. This was at a time when comics were selling for 25 cents. Little did I know that I would recreate this same process over and over again. As an adult I now focus on defaulted paper.

Graduating To The Next Level

My father was also an entrepreneur. He liked to buy airplanes. No, I am not talking about jets. Rather, I am talking about single and twin-engine airplanes. These airplanes were not new. In fact the airplanes had all been involved in serious crashes. These were planes that no one else wanted. My father was able to buy them for pennies on the dollar. I never knew exactly how much he paid, but it could not have been very much since he had to support his family on the income from his Army pay, which is very little.

My dad would take these broken airplanes and take the best pieces from each plane and put them back together into one really good plane. He spent his time on weekends putting the planes back together. I remember as a kid crawling through the tubes of the airplanes running cables from one point to another. I did not realize it at the time, but my father was teaching me how to turn trash into gold.

When the planes were completed he would lease them out to people who wanted to take flying lessons or people who wanted to rent the plane for a weekend trip. My father also liked to fly his own planes and he would take the whole family for rides. I was now about to get another lesson. On one of our rides my dad asked if I or my brother wanted to fly the plane. My brother, who is two years older, jumped at the opportunity and loved the flying. I on the other hand was terrified. I had images in my mind of plummeting the plane straight into the ground or ocean. I would not touch the controls. My father kept asking me on each trip and finally convinced me to try while I was sitting in his lap. I did not know what I was going to do. I was completely out of my comfort zone. I sat in my dad's lap. He held the controls with me and we were flying along. It was great. Then the impossible happened. He let go. I screamed. He laughed. The plane shook left and right. I thought "the end is here". Then I heard him telling me in my ear "you can do it, just believe you can". I said I don't know how. I am not as good as you are. I can't do this. He simply said do your best and "wing it". Next thing you know I was flying the plane.

I realized I did not have to know everything my dad did about airplanes. I did not have to have all of the training. That it was OK to try something and not be perfect at it. I could in fact "wing it" on almost anything.

I remember that first flying day like it was yesterday. It taught me that in order to get over my fears of doing something new or different I just had to do it. This leads me in to where I took my negotiating skills to the next level.

As I was continuing to dive for gold in the dumpsters I found other things that people threw away and started to wonder if someone would pay me money for this trash. I started to collect all of these items from the dumpster and stockpiled them in our backyard. This included furniture, clothes, pots and pans, etc. I then got my dad to rent a booth at a local flea market. I took all of my stockpiled items, put them in the back of my dad's truck and off we went to market. The table at the flea market cost $5.00. I laid everything out. While I was laying my items out on the ground for people to see, I kept wondering in the back of my mind if anyone was going to buy anything and how was I going to pay back my dad the $5.00 for the spot. That's when something amazing happened. People started to come to my area and look at things even before I had completely unloaded all I had from the back of my dad's truck. Then they were asking "how much for the pan", "how much for the bag of clothes", and on and on. At first I said 10 cents for a pan. They took it. Wow that was easy I thought. I went for 15 cents on the next item. It worked also. I kept raising the prices and they kept buying. By the end of the day I made $15 dollars and had a blast doing it. Now this was the way to make money. Over time I was doing so well that I was making between $80 - $150 each weekend at the flea market. I was rich.

The Middle Years

I have never been a person who was afraid to work hard to make money. I just discovered early on that working hard and working smart are not necessarily the same thing. I also learned that no one was going to simply hand everything to me on a silver platter. My family was not rich being in the military.

When I was 12 years old my father was killed in an automobile accident. I went to live with my mother and her husband who was also in the Army. The difference now was that instead of two boys there were now five and I was the youngest. I was last in the pecking order, which meant my older brothers already took many of the opportunities that might be available. I knew I had to make it on my own. When I was 15 my stepfather got stationed at Ft. Dix, New Jersey. He lived near his family's home in Pennington, NJ and commuted to the base for work each day.

Some of my friends came from more well to do and flat out wealthy families. To keep up I needed to generate cash. I had paper routes, cleaned gutters of leaves on houses and continued to do flea markets. I would average $100-$200 per weekend. This allowed me to purchase my first dirt bike and do some of things my wealthier friends were able to do.

In my sophomore year in high school my mother and I had a discussion about college. You see no one in our family had a college education. My mother told me that they did not have enough money to send me to college, even state school. They had a little money that could pay for my final two years of high school at a private school or use the money to pay for ½ a year at college, if they still had the money. I made the decision to attend private school and I believe it was one of the best decisions I ever made. I was an "A" student in public school. In private school I was a "C" and "B" student. When I graduated I was an "A-" student. I still did not know what I was going to do for a living.

My stepfather convinced me to join the Army. I had always told myself I would not join the Army, but here I was convinced out of fear to take the easy way out. I joined the Army right out of high school and was part of the Special Intelligence division of the Army. Even in the Army I found that I was a wheeler-dealer. I loved to make things happen and put deals together for people.

I worked with a lot of the higher brass solving problems. And boy does the military have a lot of problems.

While I was in the Army I started my college education because I had always been told that you need a college education to get a job. I was slowly falling into a trap.

After I was honorably discharged from the Army I was trying to figure out how to make more money to buy a better car, a house, go on skiing vacations, etc. At the time I was forced to live in a room in my parent's garage because I did not have enough money to get a place of my own. I got a job as an engineer, based on some of the skills I learned in the Army. I realized that in order to get ahead I needed to do something different. Everyone kept saying I would get more money and a better position if I got a university degree. So I started to go to night school. I was a full time student at night with a full time job during the day. Like I said I am not afraid of working hard if I can see the benefits down the road. Even though it looked like I was on the right track, I still felt as if something was missing. I knew I did not want this full time job. School was fun, but I did not like punching a time clock every day. So I started to look for other ways to replace the income I was making at my job.

Purely by accident I fell into the "bad" paper business. Little did I know that a simple experience would forever change my life.

Let's Start At the Beginning (Investing)…

I began in this unique business in 1985 when a friend of mine (Curtis) asked me if I would be willing to lend $2,500 to an associate in his office (Melinda), who wanted to start a business on the side. I asked Curtis to tell me a little about Melinda. He said she had been at his company for the past three years, owned her own house, a car and other assets, and that he had never heard anything negative about her in the time he had known her. He did not see any reason why she would not be able to pay me back. I told Curtis I would be happy to talk with Melinda and asked him to set up a meeting. Melinda was a very bright and intelligent woman and had a solid business plan. I thought her idea would really take off and she might make some money running the business. I asked Melinda if she would sign a promissory to pay me back the money she borrowed. She said she would be happy to sign the promissory note and it was structured to be paid in one year in 12 equal installments of $366.91. Melinda signed the promissory note and I gave her the $2,500. Payments were due on the first of the month. The first payment due date came and went. I was saying to myself, "uh-oh, this is not the best start to this business relationship. I better give Melinda a call to see if something is going on and why she has not made her first payment". I called her on the phone and said "Hi Melinda, this is Mike, remember me"? I lent you $2,500 to start a business and you signed a promissory note promising to pay me back my money. Well the first payment is now overdue. Is something going on that I need to know about?" She said she was really sorry but the contracts for her business had not come due yet but she was sure they would come in next month. I mentioned that she would have two payments plus one late fee. She said she understood that and that she would have my payment next month. I agreed and reminded her that the payment and late fee were due on the first of the month.

The second payment due date came and went. I found myself back on the phone with Melinda feeling like a broken record. She repeated that she was really sorry she was unable to make the payment, but the contracts still had not come through yet plus she had to pay for some repair work on her car. She was certain that she would be able to make the payment next month. As a matter of fact she said "Mike, I guarantee to make the payment plus all late fees next month." I said I would give her one more try and reminded her that the payments were due on the first of the month.

The third month rolled around and guess what? That's right, no check. I called Melinda again and got the same story as before except now she added that in addition to having to do more work on her car, she had to lend some money to her brother do a little landscaping along with several new excuses. All these excuses told me that she was paying everyone else on her list except me. At this point I was a little angry and frustrated. I decide it was now time to get out of this deal. I said, "I tell you what Melinda, let's forget about the interest and the late payments. Just give me back my money and I will go away". She said she could not give me back my money, she had already spent it. I asked her if she had any money in her checking or savings accounts. She said she had maybe $20. I said what about any furniture, jewelry, stereo equipment or computers that could be sold to generate some cash to give me back my money. She said she did not have anything of value. I asked her if she could borrow any money from family or friends to which she replied, "Oh no, I can't borrow money from family or friends, I won't be able to pay them back!" Obviously this was a question I should have asked in the very beginning. At this point I was a little stressed. Actually I was very stressed and frustrated, so I said to Melinda, "Look, I don't care where you get the money. Just give it back and I will go away". She said, "Mike, I am going to be very honest with you. I don't have your money and in actuality I don't plan on ever paying you back." CLICK! That's right she hung up on me. How many of you have ever watched Judge Judy on TV? Well I decided to go before the "Judge Judy" in my area, and I took Melinda to small claims court.

In the courtroom the judge asked Melinda if she signed the promissory note agreeing to pay me back my money. She said "yes your honor I signed the note but have not been able to pay because of..." and she started going over the long list of reasons why she hadn't been able to pay me back. The judge just cut her off in the middle of her sentence and slammed down the gavel saying "Judgment awarded to Mike. Warren (the plaintiff/creditor) against Melinda (also known as the debtor/defendant)".

I left the court saying, "YES! I am finally going to get my money," and expected to get paid back within the next couple of days. I went to my mailbox every day for the next two weeks looking for my check. Unfortunately, it never arrived. I figured it was possible that Melinda forgotten that she had to pay me on the judgment. So I called Melinda and said "Hi Melinda, this is Michael Warren. I'm sorry I had to take you to court. It was nothing personal. It was simply a business decision. The court did award me a judgment against you for $2,500 and you have not paid it off. I will allow you to either pay it off now or make arrangements to make payments." All Melinda said was she did not care that I had a judgment against her and that she had no intention of every paying me back and CLICK! She hung up on me again. That was twice. You would think I would have learned from the first time.

Unlike the people on those court TV shows like *Judge Judy* or *The Peoples Court*, who have their judgments paid by the TV show itself; most people don't know how to collect a judgment—even if they win the court case.

This presents a financial opportunity for you.

So there I was sitting looking at the phone trying to figure out what to do. I thought I had done everything I was supposed to do. I lent Melinda the money in good faith and she signed a promissory note promising to pay me back. She did not pay so I did what the law allowed, I took her to court, and the court agreed with me that she owed the money. Yet she still would not pay.

Then, I really thought I had the answer!

I called the court clerk where I had won the judgment and explained that I was having trouble collecting the money from Melinda and that I wanted the court to collect it for me. Guess what the court told me? Well, after the clerk stopped laughing she said, "I'm so sorry sir, but we do not collect judgments. We suggest you either collect the judgment yourself or contact an attorney to collect it for you". I said "ok, I'll do it myself, how do I collect a judgment"? The clerk said "I'm sorry sir, we cannot give you any legal advice. We suggest that you contact an attorney". So I pulled out my Yellow Pages and started calling attorneys listed in the phone book. The attorneys wanted to charge me anywhere from $300 to $1,000 in up-front fees just to attempt to collect the judgment, with no guarantee that I would get my money.

Well as you might imagine, by this time I was pretty upset. After more calls I finally found one attorney would take my case on a contingency basis. By contingency basis I mean that the attorney would not charge me any money up front. He would collect his fee only if he was able to collect money from the debtor. In return he would receive 33% of the amount collected. I said "Great! If it doesn't cost me any money up front then I really have nothing to lose. Right now I am the proud owner of a worthless judgment simply because I don't know how to go about collecting it myself."

> **To quote John D. Rockefeller,**
> **"I always tried to turn every**
> **disaster into an opportunity."**

I want to stop the story right now to explain a couple of terms so that we are all on the same sheet of music. I need you to understand the difference between a judgment, a lien and a judgment lien. We will be using these terms throughout the remainder of this book.

> ➢ **Judgment:** A legal document stating that a debt is owed from one party in a lawsuit to another party. The judgment will specify the amount of the award, attorney fees (if applicable) and the date on which interest on the unpaid balance begins.

> ➢ **Lien:** A concrete legal assertion that you have a claim of a specific value against certain property.

> ➢ **Judgment Lien:** A judgment lien is when you take a copy of the judgment and record the judgment in land records

(the same place people record mortgages and deeds.) By recording the judgment in land records you now place a lien on all property owned by the debtor within that county.

NOTE:

There are numerous other reasons judgments are obtained, including but not limited to:

- Legal services that were not paid
- Contractors not being paid
- Automobile accidents
- Rent/damages
- Medical/dental bills
- Promissory notes that were not paid
- Car leases that were not completed
- Property damage

Essentially, a judgment can occur if one person/business sues another in court and wins. A judgment is obtained and the loser can be legally forced to pay.

Back to the story...

So my attorney started the process of getting my money. The first thing he did was to place a lien against Melinda's house. By having the lien recorded this prevented Melinda from selling or refinancing her house without paying off my judgment. Then my attorney was able to use various techniques to get Melinda to pay. What I learned from this experience is that I could have also let the judgment remain attached to Melinda's house without forcing the payoff. In that case, my judgment would have gained interest at the full value. I could in essence, have treated the judgment like a bond. I invest a certain amount of money today for a specified return later. (I will go into details on how to do this in later chapters.) The moral of the story was that because Melinda owned real estate my attorney got back all of my money plus costs. The attorney kept 33% of the original $2500 for a total of $825. (We would have also collected an additional 10% in interest, which the court also appointed, if the process hadn't happened so fast.) Now I am the type of person who doesn't like to lose money. I saw that my attorney made $825 for about 1½ hours worth of work. I knew that my attorney had never appeared in court, he did everything by mail. The secret was that he knew what to do and I did not. I said to myself, "I could do this, and I can also help some of my friends who are in similar situations". So I started out collecting judgments for my friends. As I gained more experience and learned techniques to get payments faster, the more money I made.

> **This investment vehicle**
> **is not about collections**

Could you collect on judgments immediately? Sure, but let's keep it simple. I am not talking about having you go into the collection business. I am talking about you buying judgments at a discount for exceptional yields, and in most cases letting them sit attached to the debtor's real estate.

Before I go any further let me describe the mindset of the creditor and why they would sell you their judgment lien for pennies on the dollar. If you want to purchase a judgment you definitely do not want to pay the full value of the judgment. If you do pay full price, you can't make any money. You need to be compensated for buying a judgment that time has proven (to the creditor only) is unlikely to pay off to the judgment creditor. You also need to be compensated for your "future" efforts.

You should negotiate to purchase the judgment for around five to 15 cents on the dollar. So, for a $5,000 judgment, you would offer between $250 and $750. In most cases the judgment lien is already several years old. The judgment creditor believes they hold a judgment that is not collectable since the debtor has not paid it off. You might ask yourself why the creditor will sell the judgment rather than collecting the judgment themselves. There are several reasons:

- Many creditors do not know how to recover money on the judgment.
- Many creditors are also not aware that a judgment recorded in land records will attach to the debtor's property.
- Many creditors look at your offer as a guaranteed amount of cash now (which they can spend immediately) rather than the worthless document the creditor thinks they have.
- The creditor has not received any payments from the debtor since the judgment was awarded
- Most creditors are surprised to find out that they could even sell their judgments.

Purchasing judgments that are attached to real estate allow you to create a superior portfolio of paper assets that are not subject to the fluctuations of interest rates and the stock market. You buy the paper asset and let it sit in your portfolio. When the debtor eventually sells or refinances their home you get paid at full value. In order for the debtor to give clear title to a new buyer of his property, or to obtain a clear title in the event of refinancing, s/he must pay off the judgment. Most homeowners on average will stay in a house for 5-7 years before they sell or refinance. During the 5-7 years the judgment will be gaining interest at the full face value.

Did you know that you do not have to buy judgment liens at their full value?

By buying the judgment at a large discount you increase the yield on your investment. This is what we on a daily basis do for our investors at our office.

Do You Want To Be More Than an Average Investor?

My company purchased a judgment lien in that had a fair market value of $10,500. Our purchase price was $1,000 or 9.7%. We purchased the judgment with the intent to hold onto it. The judgment gained interest at the rate of 10% per year of the principal value or $1,050. Later, we received a phone call from the attorney representing the debtor. The attorney informed us that the debtor was selling his house, but unfortunately there was not enough equity to pay us off in full. He wanted to know if we would take a discount to settle the debt. The debt at this point was valued at $16,800. The most that was available to pay off this debt was $12,000. After reviewing the closing documents we agreed to settle for $12,000. Our result is that we received $12,000 on a $1,000 investment after 6 years. We made a 1,200% return on our investment and can now use the payoff funds to purchase even more liens.

On another deal, I purchased a judgment lien that had a full face value of $14,050, for just $1,219. The judgment was awarded with a court specified interest rate of 10%. With interest, court costs, and attorney's fees the judgment had a full value of almost $31,000, because it was attached to a condominium with almost $30,000 in equity. The debtor contacted us and we negotiated a payoff of the judgment at the original principal amount that was owed which was $14,050. Now you might be saying to yourself, "why on earth would you take a discount if he had a $31,000 lien attached to the property and the debtor can't sell or refinance the property without paying off the judgment?" The answer is very straightforward. In this case, the debtor was not ready to sell or refinance the property and we would have had to wait for a future payoff if I had held out. The debtor happened to catch me at a good time (somehow this always seems to be the case by the way) and I was willing to help him out since I believe everyone deserves a second chance.

> **My net result is that I had a pure profit of $12,830, which was a little over a 1000% return on my investment.**

I will explain this process in more detail and you will also learn how you can make this kind of return tax-free or at least tax-deferred.

You might be wondering, what if the debtor never contacted us or would not agree to settle, and the judgment remained in our portfolio for two more years until he decided to sell the property? This is where things start to get really interesting.

Let's look at what some of the possibilities are:

1. We buy the judgment for $1,219. The debtor does not pay off the debt for two more years (total of 10 years.) While we are waiting for the judgment to be paid the judgment is earning interest of 10% per year. (Judgments gain simple interest only-there is no compounding.)

What most people do not realize is that the debt is <u>gaining interest at the full original amount</u> of the judgment, not the discounted amount that I paid the creditor when I bought the judgment. Therefore, the judgment is gaining interest at the rate of $1,405 per year or $3.84 per day. If I receive interest income of $1,405 on an investment of $1,219 my rate of return exceeds 100% per year. So if the debtor sells the house after 10 years and pays off the judgment (let's assume the judgment is paid at full value plus interest) in the amount of $14,050 (principal), plus $2,107 (15% attorney fees), plus $14,050 (10 years of interest), for a total of $30,207. Wouldn't you say we have a very good return on our investment?

Remember, this investment did not involve the stock market. It was not subject to fluctuations in bank interest rates. And it was not subject to ups and downs in the bond market. Our investment is protected by the real property owned by the debtor. Over time the debtor will continue to make his mortgage payment, and with each mortgage payment the equity in the property increases, thereby increasing our protection in the property. Also by waiting and not having to take steps towards an immediate pay-off, we are able to defer taxes on the income until several years in the future.

2. Let's assume the debtor waits two more years before selling his home. And let's say that the housing market has not been so good and the price of the debtor's home has remained stagnant. The debtor contacts us to pay off the debt, but he wants to pay the debt at a discount.

Should you settle at a discount? I usually do, but that will be your decision. Based on your own beliefs and circumstances you might feel that you want to give the debtor a discount, especially since you paid very little for the judgment. Some of the people reading this book will want full payment while others will settle for a small or large discount. Some questions that you should consider before agreeing to discount are:

    a.   Is the debtor selling his property?

    b.   Is the property being refinanced?

    c.   Is there not enough equity in the property for full payoff?

    d.   Will the debtor pay off the judgment immediately? By paying the judgment immediately I mean within 2-3 weeks. You will want to make sure that the debtor is not "shopping" to see what kind of discount you will take, turn around and sell the house several months later and then pay you at the discounted price. Another way of saying this is that if you take a discount now, you want to be paid now and not some time in the future.

I like to have a combination of judgments that I hold for the long term and judgments that pay off fairly quickly. When a judgment lien pays off I now have the capital to go out and purchase more judgment liens, thereby growing my portfolio at a faster rate.

CHAPTER THREE

How The System Works

The system of investing in paper is very straightforward. You can use multiple techniques to find the judgment liens. To simplify this process we are going to cover the following steps:

1. Finding the paper
2. Screening the paper
3. Purchasing the paper
4. Calculating your profit when you get paid

Optional steps to take into account are how you want to purchase your investments. You should consider:

1. Personal assets versus tax-deferred investments
2. Purchasing the paper as an individual or through another entity

How To Find Your Paper

Let me describe how easy it is to find judgments and what the future holds. There are many different ways to locate judgments that are worth investigating and in my three-day live workshops I cover 15 different ways. One of the easiest methods to locate judgment liens is doing some very simple research at your local courthouse Land Records Department. First off, let me say that any courthouse research does not have to be done by you. You can hire anyone to do the research; family members, college students or people looking for part time jobs.

> **There are companies in most areas as well as on the internet that can provide you with lists of judgments. In fact the majority of all our deals are found online.**

Each courthouse contains the same information. The process you use to access the records is sometimes a little different, but you are always looking for the same information. The easiest way to understand the ins and outs of a courthouse is to just ask for help. Normally, at the entrance to the land records department (this is where the court recorded mortgages, deeds, tax liens and judgment liens are kept) is an information desk.

You could easily spend a couple of years in one courthouse and never be able to research all of the judgments available to pursue. With this in mind, it is easy to see that the judgment business is waiting for someone like you to make BIG money.

There are so many judgments to choose from!

On average, there are 350,000 judgments in every single county in the United States! And that is going back only seven years. There is one county in Illinois that has 14 million judgments, and Orange county California has over 3,000,000 judgments.

And the best news is that this is a renewable resource. On average, in every county in America <u>there are 50,000 new judgments recorded each year</u>. In Montgomery and Fairfax counties, just outside of Washington, D.C., <u>there are over 100,000 judgments filed each year</u>!

We will never have a shortage of judgments in this country because the number of law suits keeps going up and up... (see chart)

Having an abundance of judgments leads to more opportunities for you while also helping people in need. The easiest way to help out the debtor is to simply allow the debtor to pay the debt off at a discount. This is what I do most of the time and then everyone wins! The creditor wins because they receive money they thought they would never

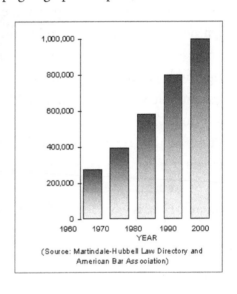

(Source: Martindale-Hubbell Law Directory and American Bar Association)

get. The debtor wins because he can pay off the debt at less than full value. You win because you make a tremendous return on your investment and your money is secured by the debtor's property.

Until the judgment is paid off the debtor is making monthly mortgage payments, thereby increasing the amount of equity in his home, which in turn increases your level of protection.

One thing is for sure... we'll never run out of judgments. There are literally billions of dollars in judgment liens just sitting there—waiting to be purchased by people who know the secrets of this business! If you do not have any money to invest yet, I have a way that could help you get started. More on this later.

Before I go any further, let me explain what this is *not.*

This is *not* a distributorship, a reseller program, or any number of the other "income opportunities" you have seen before. I'm not going to claim to do "all the work for you." What I'm proposing is to show you how you can make a lot of money in a legitimate business. It is something you learn quickly but I can't guarantee it will work for you. And I can't promise you will make a fortune. That part is up to you. All I can do is show you the simple methods that have worked for me, and other people I have taught. And while no new venture is completely foolproof, many of my students have already made thousands of extra dollars per month. Here is what some of them have to say...

"On average, I make between $1,000 and $2,000 a week in profit. On a good week I can pull in $4,000 or more. Everything Mike teaches is attainable. It just takes some common sense and the desire to learn Mike's secrets and methods."

Rod S., Tennessee

"...I have the tools and the knowledge now to become completely independent. I thank you for everything!"

Maurice G., Illinois

"...there were many great and unique ideas mentioned to fit your own personal style. Great job!"

Shirley F., New Hampshire

"Great Ideas. With these techniques, I will be making a substantial source of income."

Dan A., Illinois

"...I learned how we were actually helping the debtor; I received the confidence to go out to help others and help myself in the process."

Carol K. Canada

"I gained the ability to identify and act on opportunities that would normally have passed me by. I expect to increase my cashflow greatly."

Daniel I., Illinois

CHAPTER FOUR

How to Screen Your Investments

When looking for judgment liens you need some key information. At a minimum you should obtain the following:

1. Debtor's name
2. Debtor's address
3. Amount of the judgment
4. Date of the judgment
5. Interest rate on the judgment

All of this information can be obtained right from a copy of the judgment itself. Before you consider buying a judgment you need to determine if the debtor actually owns real estate that will act as security for your investment.

When looking at the judgment document notice the debtor's address. Let us assume that the debtor's name is John Q. Debtor who lives at 123 Main Street, Anywhere, USA. You can contact the local tax assessor's office (contact the tax assessor in the same town as the debtor's city) and ask them who owns the property at 123 Main Street. If the tax assessor tells you the owners name is John Q. Debtor you have a hit. It is that simple.

If you have a hit (the debtor owns the property that was listed on the judgment) all you need to do now is contact the creditor and attempt to purchase it.

When evaluating a judgment lien for purchase you will find that some are against individuals and some are against a business. When trying to determine which is the better purchase you should consider the following:

Person-to-Person

A person-to-person judgment is when an individual sues and wins a judgment against another individual. I believe that a person-to-person judgment is the very best type of judgment to purchase. When you send your offer letter to the judgment creditor you will have the most success with getting them to sell their judgments to you. The best types of person-to-person judgments to collect are:

- Child/Spousal (wife or husband) support
- Past due rent
- Auto accidents
- Property damage
- Services that have not been completed
- Personal loans
- Legal fees

Business-to-Person (Business)

Business-to-person judgments are the next best to pursue. A business-to-person judgment is where a business, such as "ABC Towing," sues a person or an individual who is doing business as a sole proprietor with a business name (this is known as a d.b.a. doing business as.) When analyzing these types of judgments make sure that the judgment is against a person as well as his company. If the judgment is against both the individual and his company, you can attach property owned by both the person and the business.

Business-to-Business

A business-to-business judgment is where one company sues another company in court and wins a judgment. This usually involves amounts over $5,000. Not all businesses will own property. You will have a higher hit rate if you stick with person-to-person judgment liens.

CHAPTER FIVE

How to Buy The Paper

B uying a judgment lien like most all investments is a process. You find the asset, negotiate the purchase, and hold it in your portfolio until some future date. The nice part about buying judgment liens is that you could (if you choose to) push through the payoff of the judgment anytime you want. The court system has specific procedures that allow you to collect on the judgment.

> You can pay the creditor whatever you feel the judgment is worth. Keep in mind that the less you pay for the asset (the judgment is a paper asset with the property as collateral) the lower your risk. I typically pay 5 cents to 15 cents on the dollar.

I found a judgment lien in the courthouse land records area that had a face value of $7,150. The judgment was awarded in 1995 with interest at 10%. I contacted the lien holder (creditor/plaintiff) and asked him if was interested in getting cash for his judgment, which he agreed to sell me for $1,050 or 15% of the principal value. The judgment is gaining interest at the amount of $715 per year. Since the judgment is already five years old it had accumulated interest in the amount of $3,575. The total value of the debt if it were to pay off today is $10,725. If I do nothing and just let the lien sit attached to the property gaining interest, my return on investment is 68% per year. How many people do you know that can say with confidence that their investments make 68% per year?

As another example, my wife and I recently completed the purchase of a judgment for my son (he is five years old) that was awarded in February 2000. The judgment was for $15,000. We paid $3,448.47 to purchase the judgment lien. The judgment is gaining interest at 10% per year so it makes $1,500 per year in interest. Our rate of return is 43% per year by doing absolutely nothing. The really great thing about this purchase for my son is that it was done in his ROTH IRA. That means that when the lien pays off the entire gain is tax-free. Think of what this can mean for you or your children when retirement comes along. We do not have to accept 10% or 20% mutual fund gains. Why not increase the return on your investments and best of all make them tax-free?

I also buy foreclosure properties when a good opportunity presents itself. If I am going through the trouble of doing research on a particular property I try to find as many different ways to make money from the property as possible. For example:

In doing my research on a particular property, I noticed that the property had a first trust and two judgments against it. I contacted the owner of the judgments and I agreed to purchase a $6,200 ($8150 with back interest) judgment lien for $2,300 or 28% of the judgment's full value. I purchased this judgment three days before the judgment debtor's property was scheduled for auction.

My research showed that the property was worth $275,000, but only had debt of $108,000 (first trust), another judgment for $1,200 and the judgment I purchased. My real purpose was to buy the real estate at auction, at a discount of course. My reasoning was that when the property went to auction, even if I was not the high bidder, at least the judgment would be paid off before the judgment debtor would receive any net sale proceeds. As it so happened, I was not the high bidder on the property. The property sold for $195,000. I received $8,150 from the sale proceeds of the auction. My net profit was $5,850!

You should always evaluate the debtor's property before you purchase a judgment lien. Therefore, it is important to determine the amount of equity in a property. The more equity in a property the more you can afford to pay for the judgment lien. With more equity you have extra protection (insurance) that the debtor will continue to make his mortgage payments rather than let his home go into foreclosure in an effort to avoid paying off your judgment lien.

To determine the equity in a property you first add up all of the debts. This includes a first mortgage, second and third mortgage and all other liens listed against the property. This also includes the lien you are considering for purchase. (You can ask the court clerk in the records area of your courthouse for assistance in determining the debts attached to the property.) You then determine the fair market value (FMV) of the property. Determining the FMV is as simple as calling a local real estate agent and asking them at what dollar amount the homes like your debtors are currently selling.

If you have a property with a 1st mortgage of $60,000 and a 2nd mortgage of $20,000 and a judgment lien of $10,000, you have a total debt of $90,000. You contact a real estate agent who tells you homes in the debtor's area are selling around $100,000. You take the $90,000 and divide it by the $100,000 for a debt-to-value ratio of 90%. The formula looks like this:

$$DTV = \frac{\text{Total Debt On Property}}{\text{Fair Market Value}}$$

I like to have a least 10% or more equity in the property before I consider purchasing the judgment lien. My reasoning is that if the debtor has some of his hard earned money in the property the likelihood of him not making his mortgage payments is very low.

Once you have been paid on your judgment lien you need to release the lien from the debtor's property. You do this by filing a "Notice of Satisfaction" (name varies by state.) This can all be done by mail and does not require a personal appearance in court. As always, please consult your own legal counsel for specific procedures for your state.

CHAPTER SIX

What Could Go Wrong

All investments involve some amount of risk. There is often a perceived risk and an actual risk. The difference between the two is determined by insider knowledge of how the investment works. We have all heard that the people on the inside get the best deals. Well it is also true that the people who know what other investors do not shall reap the financial gain. Do you want to wait until this investment vehicle goes mainstream and everyone is using it? You could probably guess that the investors who get started now will have the highest gains, while those investors who wait for the crowd will receive a smaller piece of the pie.

If you attempt to force the payoff of your judgment you should contact a collection lawyer to advise you on the procedures for your state. If you are not sure who to contact please visit our website at http://www.misuniversity.com. We can show you how to get low-cost legal advice in almost every state in the U.S.A. and Canada.

The risks involved with this type of investment are minimal. Even in the event of death, the lien would most likely be paid upon the sale of the estate. If the debtor filed for bankruptcy or his property was foreclosed upon, the lien would be paid as part of the sale of the home or liquidation of assets.

As was mentioned in a previous chapter you should pay as little as possible for the judgment lien. And if possible, you should also check how much equity is in the property. The more equity the higher the likelihood that you will be paid in full regardless of the circumstances.

CHAPTER SEVEN

TAX-FREE INVESTING
Financing Your Future

How do you picture your retirement? Will you be sipping a cold drink while relaxing on the balcony of your oceanfront home, secure in the comfort of your investments? Perhaps you'll be traveling through Europe while the dividend checks pile up at home. Or maybe you see yourself volunteering for your favorite cause. These don't have to be dreams. Sooner or later most of us will face the prospect of getting out of bed one morning retired. It's inevitable, and it will happen sooner than you think.

Will you have the money to live your dreams? If you are not sure, read a little further and see how the wealth building strategies of **Tax Deferred Growth or Tax Free Growth** can lead to wealth you can't imagine.

Besides looking for investment vehicles that provide us with better than averagew rates of return, how do we find ways of quantum growing our investments? What if you could make 37% or more on your money each year and do it tax-deferred or better yet tax-free? Most people would say yes. In this chapter you will learn how to combine the investment vehicle of buying judgment liens with the tax deferral benefits of retirement plans. Retirement plans can be for you, your spouse, your children or grandchildren.

We're All Getting Older

The elderly population is dramatically increasing in size. For example, the U.S. Census Bureau predicts the population above the age of 85 will double by the year 2020. Seniors 85 years of age and older will account for one-quarter to one-third of all senior citizens; as many as 27 million by the middle of the next century.

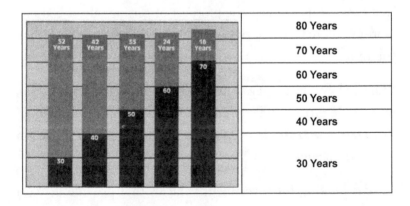

Longer life spans mean you'll need more money to sustain a comfortable lifestyle in retirement. But retirement, for the vast majority of Americans, will not be totally financed by Social

Security and pension checks. At best, Social Security will contribute *only a portion of the salaries* most people now earn.

Since 1994, joint filers with "provisional" income (adjusted gross income plus tax-exempt income, plus one-half Social Security benefits) over $44,000, pay income tax on up to 85 percent of their Social Security benefits. And as more people become eligible to collect, it is likely that Social Security benefits will be downsized even further.

The power of company pension plans has also diminished. More and more employer-financed plans are being replaced by plans in which employers match only a portion of the contributions made by their employees. Moreover, estimates are that some 20 percent of all pension funds are under-funded.

With the future of Social Security so uncertain and the first wave of baby-boomers now turning 55, and the effectiveness of company pension plans lessening, most people will have to rely heavily on their own savings and investments during their golden years.

If you are self-employed, like a growing number of people these days, you might be assuming that your booming business will provide your retirement cushion or that a regular savings account will provide the funds you will need in old age. Is that really a good idea? How can you be sure you will have the substantial financial resources you will need to make your retirement dreams come true? Obviously, systematic planning for your retirement is essential. But what are your options? One answer is to begin investing in a tax-deferred savings plan, a traditional self-directed Individual Retirement Account (IRA), or one of the newer versions such as the Roth IRA. By doing so, you'll harness *the wealth building strategies of the very rich, compound interest and tax deferral.*

> ## "You can plan for tomorrow today but you cannot plan for today tomorrow"

What Is An IRA?

First, let's cover the basics. The traditional IRA is a retirement investment vehicle originally designed to help individuals not covered by company pension plans. On January 1, 1982, the law governing IRAs was changed to make them available to anyone with earned income who also was under the age of 70½, whether or not the individual was covered by a company pension plan, profit sharing plan, or a 401(k), all of which are known as qualified plans. Remember, everyone with earned income can have an IRA and at the time of this writing invest up to $4,500 every year.

An IRA Combines
The Most Powerful Forces On Earth -
Compound Interest & Tax Deferral

Compound Interest

When asked, "What is the most powerful force on earth?" Albert Einstein replied without hesitation, "compound interest!" And more than 200 years ago Benjamin Franklin defined the concept as "the stone that will turn all your lead into gold." How does it work? It is simply earning interest on your interest, as well as your principle.

Let's take a look at 40 years of compounding for two, twenty-five year olds. The first person makes a $2,000 investment for each of the first 10 years, while the second person waits until the 11th year to make a contribution and then continues for the next 30 years. Each portfolio compounds at 10%.

Year	Annual Contribution	Ending Balance	Annual Contribution	Ending Balance
1	2,000	2,200	0	0
2	2,000	4,620	0	0
3	2,000	7.282	0	0
4	2.000	10,210	0	0
5	2.000	13,431	0	0
6	2,000	16.974	0	0
7	2,000	20,872	0	0
8	2.000	25,159	0	0
9	2,000	29,875	0	0
10	2,000	35.062	0	0
30	0	235,886	2,000	126,005
31	0	259,470	2,000	140.806
32	0	285,417	2,000	157.086
33	0	313,959	2.000	174.995
34	0	345.355	2,000	194,694
35	0	379,890	2,000	216,364
36	0	417,879	2.000	240,200
37	0	459,667	2,000	266,420
38	0	505,634	2,000	295,262
39	0	556,197	2,000	326,988
40	0	611,817	2,000	361,887
Total	$20,000	611,817	$60,000	361,887

As astounding as it may seem, the person who invested less money, but did so at the beginning of the compounding period, actually has over 50% more money than the person who invested three times as much.

Compound Interest With Tax Deferral

> ### Success Story
> An investor in the Southwest ran out of money for his real estate rehabs. What he did next was very creative. He bought a house for $30,000, which included $5,000 for fix-up, using money from other investor's IRAs. He paid them 15% ($2,250) for 6 months, for the use of their money. He sold the house for $52,000. After paying his investors, he had a gain of $19,750!

With some exceptions discussed later (see the section on ROTH IRA's to see how to earn tremendous returns tax-free), IRAs defer all taxes until money is withdrawn during your retirement. This means that you compound growth much faster than if you had to pay current taxes. The longer an IRA is kept going, the more this power can work to increase the value of your investments.

Let's look at two examples. First, a self-directed IRA is set-up and funded with $2,000. Every year thereafter an annual contribution of $2,000 is made on January 1st. Assuming the IRA is earning a positive return, it will combine the magic of compound interest with tax deferral.

Nobody knows what interest rates will do in the future. But if your IRA earned a constant 10 percent return, after 10 years your total $20,000 investment would already be worth $35,000, a $15,000 gain. After 25 years your $50,000 invested would be worth $216,000. In 35 years your $70,000 investment would be worth $596,000, a gain of $526,000!

Use Other Peoples IRAs Like Your Own Private Bank

Some creative investors use the IRAs of other people they know. They pay them a good rate of interest for the use of their money or they share a percentage of the profits.

Anything you can do in your own IRA account can be done in someone else's IRA. If you need money to fund your deals, get your doctor, lawyer or other professional friends and associates to open self-directed IRAs at an approved IRA custodian. The example I described earlier where I bought a judgment lien with my son's Mid-Ohio Securities ROTH IRA is one way to fund your deals. The twist is that the proceeds of the judgment lien are going into my children's IRA, which will help provide for their financial future.

Tax Deferred, Compounded Growth

The key to a traditional IRA's great power as a financial tool is that all of its income, interest, dividends, and profits are exempt from taxation until a withdrawal is made. This gives it a great edge over investments that pay taxes.

Imagine buying judgment liens in your IRA or your child's IRA. The entire accumulated return on the judgment lien can be used to purchase other judgment liens without having to pay your taxes. Essentially, you can get an additional 30%-50% to use towards future purchases.

In my three-day live seminars I show people how they can invest just $1,000 for seven years and make a cash return of close to $119,000. Let me explain. At the end of seven years I am making the assumption that interest has accumulated at the full amount for each lien over the seven year period. In my workshops I go over the exact detail calculating the interest and what is referred to as the time value of money. But for my example and illustration we will make these assumptions so that you can understand what it is that we are trying to accomplish.

Over the next year you find just one lien each year that has a value of $10,000 (see chart on next page). You use your IRA, ROTH IRA, or other pension plan to purchase the judgment liens for $1,000 or 10% of the principal value. The creditor was very happy to get something for the judgment, especially since the creditor thought it was worthless. The judgment only appears worthless because the creditor does not know that the judgment debtor cannot sell or refinance the house without paying off the debtor.

If you purchase one judgment lien each year over the next seven years you will have invested $7,000. The total principal value of the judgment liens you have purchased equals $70,000 (7 x $10,000). Assuming all of the judgments gained interest at the same rate of 10% per year. Each judgment lien gains interest at the full value of $1,000 (10% x $10,000). Multiply the $1,000 in interest times the seven judgments and you have $7,000. Multiply the $7,000 times seven years and you have accumulated interest of $49,000. Now what would happen if all of the judgments happened to pay off in the same year? You would have a cash payout (into your IRA) of $119,000. This is only after 7 years. With these kinds of numbers you could quantum leap the value of your retirement plans. Even if you got started late on saving with a retirement plan, investing in judgment liens can provide you with a means to make up for lost time. After the judgment liens pay off you now have $119,000 to purchase more judgment liens. How many could you purchase now?

Doing The Numbers

$10,000   @   10%   = $1,000/year in interest

Principal	Interest
$10,000	$1,000
x 7 (judgments)	x 7 (judgments)
$70,000	$7,000
	x 7 (years)
	$49,000

Totals: $70,000   Return: $119,000/$7,000 = 1,700%
        + $49,000   return on your investment
        $119,000

Non-Mandatory Contributions

By law, you may contribute to your IRA up to 100 percent of the first $2,000 that you earn each year. If a husband and wife are working they can both establish an IRA and contribute up to $2,000 per year for a family total of $4,000. Non-working spouses are eligible for a spousal IRA, and $2,000 per year can be invested in these accounts. There is no mandatory requirement for making a contribution every year.

Here's another point to remember. You don't have to contribute to your IRA plan at the same time as you open your account. You can fund your account with as little as $200-$500 and then contribute from $0-$2,000 annually. There is no requirement that you have to contribute $2,000. Some people have made great profits with just a little money invested.

You have until April 15th each year to make the contribution for the previous tax year. You might think it is advantageous to wait until the last minute to make your IRA contributions but waiting can actually be a mistake. The earlier you make your contributions each year, the more time this money will have to grow and the more time it will be protected from taxes. The longer you continue contributing to an IRA, the greater the immediate savings on your income tax.

Even if you're not in the highest tax brackets, these savings can be impressive over even a relatively short time span. Putting your money into an account January 1st each year, compounding an extra 15½ months, instead of April 15th of the next year, could be worth more than $54,000 to you, over the life of your IRA earning just 10%.

> **If you risk nothing,
> you risk everything!**

How To Make Your Child Or Grandchild A Millionaire

There are compelling reasons why your child, grandchild or other young relative should have an IRA:

- You can transfer your assets to your children while you're still alive.
- If employed, your child or grandchild will get a tax deduction.
- Their money compounds tax deferred for 20, 50 even 100 years.
- It will create estates for your children and grandchildren and make them millionaires.
- The company that hires them gets a tax deduction.

> IRS rule:
> There is no minimum
> age to have an IRA.

Begin by investing $2,000 per year for four years when your child is 10, an $8,000 total cash investment. Compound this amount at 10 percent and it would amount to $1,089,000 by the time the child reaches age 65; compound at 12 percent, and the total would equal $2,762,000! The same $2,000 investment made for eight years - a $16,000 total cash investment would amount to $2,017,000 when compounded at 10 percent, and $5,059,000, compounded at 12 percent!

In reality though, no one knows what tax rates will be in 69 years. Here's a solution. Start a Roth IRA, rather than a traditional IRA, for your child. This new IRA has a unique feature. While there is no deduction from current income taxes for the contribution (and your child won't need one), there are also no taxes imposed when the money is withdrawn during retirement years. In the above example, your child would get to keep the whole 1.4 million dollars. *Not bad for a $2,000 one time investment!*

I opened ROTH IRA's for both of my children. I look for judgment liens to purchase with the assets in their IRA. As the trustee of the IRA I can make the investments on behalf on my children. Once the assets are purchased, I have the option of forcing the payoff or letting it sit in my child's IRA, gaining interest at the full face value until it pays off when the homeowner (debtor) refinances or sells his home.

Many People Ask, "How Can I Employ My Children?"

If you employ your child or grandchild in the family business, the child can earn income of $2,000 (maximum amount allowed into the IRA per year) and the business would get a deduction for $2,000. The child is now eligible to open an IRA. The contribution can be deducted from the child's income, so there is no income tax to pay. Please note I am not an accountant or attorney and I am not providing any legal or accounting advice. Please seek competent legal advice before implementing.

For a business sole proprietorship, no FICA (Social Security) is paid if the child is under 18 years of age and no FUTA (unemployment) is paid if the child is under 21 years of age. If incorporated however, FICA and FUTA must be paid no matter what the child's age. If the business is a partnership and the parent is the only partner, the child would be treated as a sole proprietorship.

One creative way to have children earn income is to use their photographs to advertise your business. You can pay them $2,000 per year for the rights to use their photographs in your business advertising. Just have some professional pictures taken at a studio and you're on your way. This is a simple way to put money into your child's IRA and make it tax deductible to you or your business. Taking this example, the final step entails buying the rights to the photographs each year. This means that you can make you child's IRA grow by a new contribution of $2,000 each and every year.

Here's another twist on this idea. Why not have your child's IRA buy equipment that is used in business? The business can then lease that equipment from the IRA. Not only does the business get a deduction when it purchases the rights to the photographs which established the IRA in the first place, the business now gets to deduct the equipment leasing costs as a business deduction too!

What To Look For in An IRA Custodian

Many IRA custodians and trustees will not permit IRAs to own interest in the kinds of investments that some successful investors now utilize. These are permitted investments under Federal law. Many professionals in the financial services field, who haven't taken the time to read the law, assume that these investments are not permitted. This is not true. The first thing to look for is the IRA's ability to be "self-directed." Self directed means you get to choose exactly what investments you want to purchase with your IRA money. As the Trustee for my children's ROTH IRAs, I am able to purchase assets on their behalf.

You Don't Have To Settle For Underachieving Investments!

- Low Interest Rate CDs
- Poor Performing Stocks, Bonds or Mutual Funds
- Unsatisfactory Insurance Products

Make sure your IRA custodian allows you to invest or own an interest in:

- Private Corporations
- General Partnerships
- Limited Liability Companies
- Limited Partnerships
- Land Trusts
- Public Corporations

Through these types of entities you could purchase judgment liens for you and your family while deferring the taxes.

At a minimum you should check the custodian's history of customer services and if there have been any complaints filed against them.

Mid-Ohio Securities understands what a judgment lien is and the returns that can be made with them. That was a primary requirement for me to move funds to their firm.

Why A Self-Directed IRA Is A Great Investment

- It cuts your tax bill each year.
- It shelters the interest, dividends, income and profits that your IRA earns until you're ready to start withdrawing money, which may be any time between ages 59½ and April 1 following the year in which you become 70½. (At that time you must start withdrawing). The longer these tax deferred earnings keep piling up, the bigger the retirement fund it will build.
- It's completely under your control. You decide where to invest your money and can count on having it when you retire or decide to use it for any other purpose. No matter how often you change jobs, your IRA will stay with you, making it especially useful for people who change jobs often.

- You don't have to contribute each year if you can't afford to or don't want to. As far as the IRS is concerned, you can put as much or as little in your IRA (or IRAs) as you wish so long as you don't exceed the annual contribution limits.
- You can switch investments from one IRA to another as your circumstances change.
- You have great flexibility in adapting to changes in your income or financial circumstances during the crucial years between ages 59½ and 70½. If you're still earning compensation, you can continue contributing to your IRA during these years even though you're making withdrawals.
- It can be inherited by anyone (or any number of people) you designate if you die before the money in the IRA is exhausted. If your spouse is your designated beneficiary and you die before distributions from your IRA have begun, your spouse may delay taking distributions until they reach age 70½.
- If you own a business you can set up an IRA for yourself without having to include your employees, which you must do with a Keogh, SEP or the new SIMPLE IRA plan. If however, you are the only employee of your company, then these other plans will work for you too.
- Although you may have to pay penalties for taking money out before you are age 59½, an IRA provides easy access to funds in an emergency. If the money has been compounding tax deferred in the IRA long enough, even with the penalty, your overall return may be higher than on taxable investments of comparable safety.
- The self-directed IRA plan offers the greatest variety of investment selection giving you the greatest flexibility and control. You invest your money in the things you are most comfortable with.

> *"Forever is a long time*
> *but not as long as it was yesterday."*

The New Roth IRA

The Roth IRA created in the summer of 1997 and effective January 1st, 1998, was designed to avoid the payment of taxes at the time of distribution, provided you meet certain requirements.

Many experts feel that because of this feature, it is destined to become the most popular savings plan. Here is a summary of the features of the Roth IRA:

- An individual may contribute a maximum limit of $2,000 each year.
- Any contributions to a Roth IRA and a traditional IRA may not exceed a combined total of $2,000.
- Contributions made to a Roth IRA are allowable if they meet the criteria listed on the next page.
- Contributions to Roth IRAs can be made after age 70½.
- Unlike traditional IRAs, there is no mandatory distribution required when you reach age 70½.
- A major distinction between the Roth and a traditional IRA is that the contribution to a Roth is not tax deductible. This is offset by allowing for *tax-free distribution* later on.

The new law allows for a rollover or conversion from a traditional IRA. This issue will be discussed later in this report under the section called, "Rollover From A Traditional IRA To A Roth IRA."

I recently purchased another lien that was originally awarded for $5,000. I split up the ownership of the judgment between my son and my daughter so they each own a 50% share of the judgment lien. Approximately one month after the purchase, I was contacted by a mortgage company asking me for a payoff amount. A week later we received a check for $12,954. This money is split equally between my children. The result is a net profit of almost $11,000 tax-free (tax free since the lien is owned by their ROTH IRAs).

> **"Retirement takes all the fun out of Saturdays"**

Rollover From a Traditional IRA To a Roth IRA

This is an idea that will require a lot thinking and planning on the part of an IRA owner.

The new law allows for a rollover from a traditional IRA to a Roth for all individuals or couples with a Modified Adjusted Gross Income (MAGI) of less than $100,000. For married individuals filing separately, no rollover is allowed. Here are some of the features and benefits of this rollover plan:

- Any amount rolled over from a traditional IRA to a Roth, will not be subject to a 10% premature distribution penalty.
- However, the full amount will be taxable; that is, the amount of the rollover must be added to your income. For rollovers made in 1998, this tax can be paid over a four-year period. Rollovers made after 1998 will be fully taxed in the year of the rollover.

> **"In Two Days, Tomorrow Will Be Yesterday"**

How Long Can An IRA Last

An IRA could last 100 years or more. Take the example of a 35-year-old man. His IRA account compounds tax deferred until he reaches age 70½. That's 35 years. Shortly thereafter he dies. His spouse who is 70½ inherits the IRA and lives until age 80½. That is another 10 years.

Finally, the couple's beneficiary inherits the IRA at the age of 35. Assuming he or she lives their full life expectancy, (age 85), that adds another 55 years to the previous total of 45 years. That's a grand total of 100 years. And even though some distribution occurs, tax deferred compounding applies to the income and profits earned during all of these 100 years.

Ultimately, using your IRA to invest in judgment liens is great opportunity to combine the benefits of tax-free growth with above average returns. Even if you do not have an IRA set up, it is not too late. For the simple reason that you can double or triple your investments in a matter of years while having your assets secured by real estate. Put another way, you can make up for lost time but you need to get started now.

CHAPTER EIGHT

Be Like Mike

Picture a profitable business with employees and nice office, company car, paid vacations around the world, respected in the community. Is this you? Can you imagine yourself running your own successful business? If you can I am about to share with you some rock solid principals for forming a business to profit from the defaulted paper industry. If you want to copy what I have done and create a company that does the work for you then you will love this chapter. I am going to show you how to be like Mike (that's me). I am going to start out by covering some of the basics. I will share with you how I got started and what I am doing today. I am sure you will find it as interesting to read as I have found it to be when I wrote it.

Going To The Next level

Whenever I do seminars, I am always approached by people wanting to know how they can go to the next level and duplicate what I have done. Some investors decide that they want to take buying Bad Paper to a whole new level and hire employees and create a full-fledged company.

I have also found that some investors are perfectly happy with doing one or two deals a month, which provides them with a very nice income. In chapter eight I will show you what happens with your income and how you can grow your money very quickly so that you can make as much as you want without a lot of effort on your part.

So, how do you create a company from scratch? I want to be very clear on what I am about to say. It takes careful planning. But the rewards are great. You no longer have to do all of the work yourself. The single biggest mistake I see investors make is to get so caught up in the details of forming a company they forget why they are a creating a company in the first place. The original goal was to buy paper, but to do it on a larger basis. Don't fall into "paralysis by analysis". Just get started.

Our economy is no longer conducive to the huge corporate organization. That age has passed its peak, and the American business world is in a phase of serious "downsizing." The fact is this process of downsizing has already thrown tens of thousands of former corporate players out of the office high rise and into smaller businesses. Many others have decided to leave the towers of corporate America because they've had enough, or because they see the handwriting on the wall. Many of these people are simply doing on their own what they did as employees, but now they're doing it as consultants or private contractors.

No one feels secure about "corporate security" anymore. Corporate cutbacks and downsizing have thrown tens of thousands of top corporate players out into the cold. This has made it more stressful for the managers who remain. They have to do more, faster.

So is starting a defaulted mortgage business really difficult? No. At least not if you follow some basic guidelines and considerations. You might ask yourself why should I start a business anyway?

Benefits of Having Your Own Business

When I got started I did not have a clue about what I was doing. I learned everything by trial and error. I did not even know if I should start and official company, so I just got started on my own. I started in a room in my parent's garage. It did not even have a bathroom. I had to walk across the yard and go into my parent's house to take a shower and brush my teeth. I was the president, accountant, sale person, marketing person and cleaning crew. I did everything. Creating a business means you can have other people do these positions for you so that you can focus on the strategic planning or whichever part of the business you like the most.

Short Commute

Of the many advantages of doing business at home, one of the biggest is one of the most obvious: it's a short commute.

In fact, the commuting time to most home offices - unless the home is incredibly large - is under one minute. You simply walk down or up some stairs, or down a hall, and voila! – you're at the office. There is no hassling with getting into cold cars on wintry mornings, fighting traffic as time flies and blood pressure rises, finding (and paying for) urban parking that is getting to be as scarce as it is expensive, and negotiating a gauntlet of people, elevators, and knots of workers to get to where the work actually gets done. And there's no reversing the same grueling process to get home.

It is not uncommon for a worker in the suburbs to spend an hour getting from his kitchen table to his office desk each morning. In Los Angeles and certain other metropolitan areas, that figure can be more than doubled. Some people actually spend four to five hours each business day getting to and from work.

Commuting is not only hard on your schedule and patience; it's also a killer when it comes to auto expenses. When you think of what a car costs to run per mile (cost of car itself, insurance, taxes, registration, fuel, maintenance, perhaps tolls, etc.), you can get ulcers just watching the speedometer turn over. Home office workers don't even use their cars to get to and from work. This translates to significant savings.

Loose Dress Codes

Typical dress standards for the home-based office are as loose as last night's pajamas. Because many home business operators don't get visits from customers, clients, or associates in the course of the working day - or do so only rarely - they

> **YOUR FOUNDATION OF SUCCESS**
>
> Making yourself a successful home business owner and making a lot of money are not necessarily the same things.
>
> You can make a boatload of money, but if you're not a "successful person," chances are good that you'll lose it or misuse it. If you are a "successful person," however, you'll have the knowledge, skills, and discipline to move steadily toward the goal of financial freedom, and having once achieved it, you'll keep it and enhance it.

can dress however they wish to dress - even naked if that's their inclination.

Home office attire is clearly more comfortable than the suit-and-tie dress codes of the corporate tower - just another advantage of working at home.

Home With The Family

There is a trend, especially among baby boomers that are now raising their own babies, which has been referred to as "cocooning." It involves staying home with the family rather than rushing from place to place outside the home in hot pursuit of money and pleasure. One of my important considerations when I do business is how is it going to affect my family?

It makes a decided difference to a household to have at least one of the parents working at home, in contrast to having both. Home-based businesses fit perfectly into the mentality that finds its expression in cocooning - an attitude of home, family, and quiet togetherness parents away at an office during the day. Even though the "homey" is busy and involved in work, he or she is still there to handle emergencies and crisis situations. Just the presence of a parent in the house creates a feeling of supervision and security.

Tax Breaks

Having an office in the home is one of the few remaining tax breaks available to the taxpayer.

If you use part of your home regularly and exclusively as an office, many of the expenses may be deductible. However, you can't deduct more than the net amount of income you generate by using the home office. Just check with your accountant for details on your situation.

Considerations When Forming Your Business

The first thing you must decide when creating a business is what is it the business is supposed to do and how will the business accomplish its tasks.

When I was starting out in business over 15 years ago I did not have a clue on what I was doing or how I should go about it. I just jumped in and hoped for the best. Well I want to take the time to explain a few things to you so that you will not run into the same roadblocks that I did.

The first thing that you should do, and thankfully I did do this part, is to set your goals? This is often easier said than done. Most people look at setting a goal as deciding what you want (money, time, cars, boats, etc.) from the effort you put out. The challenge comes in making the goal specific so that you can obtain what you want in a reasonable time period. So how do you do it? You create a blueprint for your goals.

Which Form To Choose For Your Business

Going into business for yourself may be only one of many dreams you have. You may just want to be your own boss. Maybe you want to get the kids through college. Maybe you just want to make more money. Whatever your plans, it's important to consider carefully the form your business will take. You should decide which form you will use before you print any business cards, or stationary. The forms your business can take are listed in order of least complex to most complex. Many of our students start out just like I did, as a sole Proprietorship, and as their business generates income they convert it to a corporation.

Sole Proprietorship

The simplest form of business. You are the sole owner. The buck stops there.

If you own a sole proprietorship, you will need to fill out a Schedule C federal income tax form when you do your yearly taxes. The income you make from your business is included with any other income you made that year. If you make money you will have a certain amount of tax that you must pay. On the other hand running a business also means that you generate expenses. These expenses are deductible against any money you made that year.

Advantages
- Little to no bureaucratic red tape involved
- Least expensive to set up
- Tax? You and the business are the same
- Business losses will offset gains from other income sources

Disadvantages
- All responsibility for everything rests on your shoulders
- For liability purposes, you and the company are the same

This is a very important thing to consider. For instance, as the sole proprietor, if you face a reversal of fortune because of ill health or some other unforeseeable circumstance, your creditors will still have rights to your money.

As I gained more experience and made more money I realized that I wanted to protect myself. One of the easiest ways to protect yourself is with a corporation or a partnership. So I embarked on a mission to learn as much about asset protection as I could. Asset protection simply means protecting what I have for the benefit of my family. Simple steps give me the comfort of running a business without any worries.

Partnerships

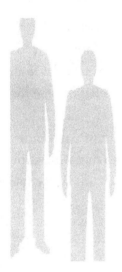

Partnerships fall between sole proprietorships and corporations (but closer to sole proprietorships) in terms of complexity and governmental regulations. You can have a legal partnership without even writing up articles of partnership, though it's wise to do so. All you basically need to do to launch this type of business is apply for any required business permits and start operations.

Although most home businesses are "one-person shops," it is not uncommon to find those that have two or more partners, including people who live together and those that do not.

The definition of a partnership, according to The Uniform Partnership Act (which has been adopted by many states), is an association of two or more persons to carry on as co-owners of a business for profit." Let's take a look at two types of partnerships:

1. General Partnership
2. Limited Partnership

General Partnership

This is where two or more people are decision-making owners in the business.

Advantages

1. The General partnership is pretty simple.
2. You and your partners are equals. You share equally in the management and the profits.
3. You have the benefit of your partner's financial resources, skills and abilities instead of just your own.
4. No one new can join the partnership without permission of all the partners.
5. You don't need a contract between you and your partners, but one is advisable.

Disadvantages

1. You will also share in the responsibility if one of the partners signs a $500,000 contract on behalf of the company, even if you gave explicit instructions not to!
2. Each partner is taxed on his share, whether or not the money was distributed during the year.

Limited Partnership

In this arrangement, there are two kinds of partners, General and Limited. The General Partner has the same advantages and disadvantages as in a General Partnership.

The Limited Partner is more like a stockholder. His liability is limited to his investment in the business. However, this partner cannot be involved in the management of the company. If he does get involved, he is considered more like a general partner.

Limited Partnerships are normally formed in conjunction with real estate companies for tax advantages.

Advantages

1. Allows access to additional financing through the limited partners.
2. Can have general partners as well as limited partners thereby gaining advantages of both forms of business.

Disadvantages

1. There is a lot of additional paperwork involved.
2. As a general partner you still have all the disadvantages of a general partnership.

Partnerships are not taxed on their income. Instead, the income (or losses) "pass through" to the individual partners and are taxed as income to them at their own individual tax rate. This is similar to the way things are handled in a sole proprietorship, except that additional tax forms must be filed come tax return time.

Partners must show their partnership income as personal income on form 1040 when completing their annual tax returns. Like the other business structures, the partnership can offset its income by allowable deductible business expenses.

Corporation

This is by far the most complex of all the business structures. Home business owners that form corporations do so generally to take advantage of a major benefit of this type of structure: limitation of liability. The downside of having a corporation is the added burden and expense of regulations and red tape, and in some instances, the double taxation that hits a corporation.

Corporations are typically formed under the authority of a state government. Creating a corporation is not as quick and easy as forming a sole proprietorship or partnership. Creating a corporation is not difficult. I can pick up any newspaper today (like the Wall Street Journal or USAToday) and find ads for companies that provide a service to do all of the paperwork for you. I highly recommend this method. It saves you a lot of time, especially if you are not sure what forms need to be filed in your stat. These companies know all of the rules, regulations and fees associated with creating a corporation. I have formed a corporation in as little as 24 hours. I simply pick up the phone, tell them the name of the company I want to forma and the state (yes you can have a corporation that is formed in another state) I want it created. 24 hours later I am in business. Not difficult at all. The formation company provides me with all of the documents that I need to correctly fun my business. I also get a corporate seal and stock certificates (if I want to sell stock to someone at a later date).

There are two main types of corporations. A "C" corporation and a "subchapter S corporation". The "subchapter S corporation," commonly known as simply the "S corporation" has become popular because it offers shareholders (owners of the company) the liability limitations of a corporation, and yet allows income and losses to pass through to the shareholders without being taxed at the corporate level. This means you get all of the benefits of a full-fledged corporation, but you are only taxed at your own individual tax rate.

In many ways a corporation is the ideal business form even if your business is very small. Corporations are not necessarily giant companies with offices in many states. They can be tiny companies of one or two people (often referred to as "Closely Held"). Using this business form can be a very smart move on your part.

A Closely Held Corporation does not sell stock like a Public Corporation that is listed on the New Your Stock Exchange. It is made up of just a few people, (or possibly just yourself alone!) who are all involved in the day-to-day operations of the business to one degree or another.

Advantages

1. Depending on your state of incorporation you may have as few as one person in your corporation.
2. Limited liability. The corporation is separate from you.
3. The business continues intact even if the owner dies. Ownership of the company is easily transferred.
4. Fewer rules and regulations

Disadvantages

1. More paperwork and bureaucracy involved
2. Personal Collateral may still be necessary to get loans
3. Initial cost of incorporation. (costs range from around $100 -$600 depending on the state of incorporation)

Incorporation fees vary from state to state, however you may always consider incorporating your business in another state, such as Nevada, where the laws favor small businesses. There are many sites on the Internet that can help you form a corporation at the least possible cost. If you don't have Internet access, simply look in the back of the Wall Street Journal or USA Today newspaper

Be sure to do your homework concerning the requirements of out-of-state corporations doing business in your home state.

Corporate Taxation

Because the subject of corporate taxation is far too complex to deal with here, we'll simply say that a corporation is taxed differently than a partnership or a sole proprietorship because the corporate entity itself is taxed on corporate income, and then the shareholders are taxed on the income they receive from their shares in the corporation. In the sole proprietorship and the partnership, the business entities themselves are not taxed since all profits are passed to you directly.

You can own a corporation and have the corporation hire you as an employee to manage it. The corporation pays you a wage and provides company-paid benefits, such as health insurance. The wages and benefits are tax deductible to the corporation. You pay taxes on the wages you receive. T he corporation pays corporate taxes on the profits that remain after paying you for your wages and benefits. I like this form of corporation because I am able to pass a lot of expenses to the business that I would not be entitled to as a sole proprietor. For instance I can have my company lease a fancy car. The lease is fully deductible to the company as an expense. I can also have my company pay for my travel to do research for defaulted mortgages in different parts of the country.

This situation applies to the regular corporation (C corporation), but not to the S corporation. The S corporation is not taxed as a business entity. Rather, the income or losses pass through to the shareholders, where they are taxed as personal income, just as happens in the sole proprietorship and the partnership.

Once you have decided what form your business will take, you will need to begin the process of licensing, registering and the actual legal steps necessary to properly set up your business.

Legal Requirements

Always consult your attorney. I am not a lawyer or accountant. Therefore by law I cannot give you any legal or accounting advice. I can however give you my personal opinion.

A smart business owner knows when to defer to an expert. If you have questions about your books, taxes, contracts, rights or your liability, get the appropriate professional help.

<u>Licensing</u>

To do business you need to have a business licensee. The license is a means for the appropriate government agencies to register your company to help assure that your actions are legal and the appropriate taxes are paid. Licensing has the advantage of lending a great deal of credibility to your business. Potential clients will be more likely to trust you and feel comfortable about doing business with you. Don't let this frighten you. It's not a big deal. Most business licenses are fairly inexpensive-for instance in Colorado it only costs $8

As a bad paper investor who buys for his own portfolio you do not need any type of a specialty license such as a mortgage broker would need. Since you actually become the owner of the judgment, which you find, regulations that apply to mortgage brokers and debt collectors do not apply to you. However, obtaining a simple business license will give you credibility and legitimacy that you would not have otherwise. On a side note you need to verify if your state requires any licensing in order to resell bad paper. Usually this license is not difficult to obtain.

To get your business license you should contact your local licensing agency. There is usually a small fee for the license. If you need help finding the correct agency, call your local chamber of commerce listed in your phone book.

Naming Your Business

Give some thought to this decision. The name of your business is often the first image a potential client has of you. And again, first impressions are lasting impressions. You may want to get some outside input for this. Sit down with your spouse or another relative and brainstorm. Call up your friends and get their help. A catchy name can help potential clients remember you. It should convey:

- Reliability
- Creativity
- Professional Ability
- Trustworthiness

If you are a Sole Proprietorship you have three options.

1. **Use your own name.**

   The advantage is you do not have to jump through any legal hoops or go to any time and expense to use it. You might want to use your name is if the public already recognizes it. In other words you are a famous movie star, sports figure, or beloved political figure. However, that last one may be impossible to attain and the others leave most of us out.

2. **Set up a DBA.**

   This stands for "Doing Business As". Officially the business is your actual name but checks can be written out to the DBA name and still cashed. If you chose this it may be a good idea to take the third step and register the DBA as a trade name when you can afford it.

3. **Register a trade name.**

   This is the most involved but also protects you to a greater extent. A good name is a valuable asset and registering it as a trade name assures that you will not lose it.

Federal Employer Identification Number

Sole proprietors who are not employers usually do not have to apply for a Federal Employer Identification Number (EIN), unless they engage in certain types of business activities.

All other business entity types must apply for this registration whether they have employees or not. For more information on this registration, call the IRS at 1-800-829-1040 or check out the IRS website online.

A recent change at the IRS allows you to apply for your number by faxing form SS4 to the IRS. You can receive your EIN within 5 days to 6 weeks. That is the standard time frame the IRS will give you on when to expect your EIN. I have, however received my EIN numbers back in as little as three days.

In most cases to open up a business checking account you will need this number. If you do not have an EIN number tell the bank it is applied for or use your social security number as a means of identification until you receive your official EIN.

Developing your Business Image.

Your success as a business is going to depend a great deal on your ability to attract clients or customers. This will be a function of the quality and professionalism you portray in your business image. Remember, first impressions are lasting impressions.

Let your guiding motto be "Classy but not flashy". It is possible to go overboard with your image. I always think back to a commercial that I saw where tennis ace Andre Agassi made what I considered a very profound statement: "Image Is Everything". Protect your image.

What You Can "Not" Do

As far as the legalities of your business name, if you are incorporated in any way, you must register a trade name, and it must include the words Corporation, Company or the initials Inc.

It is prohibited or restricted to use terms such as "medical" "national" "bank" "insurance" or "trust" in your company name.

Most states will reject a name that closely resembles one already on file. You may do a name search on a statewide basis, however, you may wish to obtain the services of an attorney if you want to do a name search on a national level.

NOTE

Names like <u>Bob's Funding</u> or <u>Annie Enterprises</u> don't convey an image of maturity or reliability. Annie sounds friendly, but not too serious. Bob sounds as if he still hasn't made up his mind what his company does. Names of this type sound as if they're running the business out of the spare bedroom. Even if they are, they don't need to convey that message in the company name.

Business Stationary

You will need to choose a font style, ink color or colors, a paper, and possibly a logo. Creativity is a valuable asset to have at this stage of the process. If you are not very creative, consider hiring a professional graphic designer. If you cannot afford this, ask to borrow a copy of some stationary and business cards from local businesses. Follow their example.

Utilize the services of your local copy shop. Many of them have computers and laser printers they can rent in the store. Kinko's is a perfect example of this service. If you are familiar with the programs and take some time to think it out first, you can save a lot of money by doing it yourself

Phone Etiquette

A portion of your business will be conducted over the phone. Potential clients paint a mental picture of you when they talk to you on the phone. If you smile when you talk, they will be able to hear it in your voice. A helpful tool I use is to have a mirror next to the phone. When you are on the phone look in the mirror. If you have a smile on your face it will come across in your voice.

Pay particular attention to the answering machine message. When people call you after hours they should get a professional sounding message giving them the option of leaving a recorded message for you. There is no need to be humorous or lengthy. Identify your business, thank them for calling, and let them quickly leave a message for you.

Marketing

An important ingredient of every successful business is to have an effective marketing strategy. However, it is easy for a business to spend its profits and then some on ineffective advertising. I can personally attest to this statement. I have wasted thousands of dollars over the years marketing in areas that produced little if even response. Therefore it is imperative that you to be very selective in your approach to advertising. Do NOT spend big dollars when you are just starting out. If you are like I was you typically have more time than money. Use your time instead of your hard earned money. Make face-to-face contact with referral sources instead of advertising in the newspaper. One of the most effective places to get referrals for Bad Paper is an attorney. Set up face-to-face meetings with the attorneys and get to know them and let them get to know you, what you do and how it can help their client get some much needed cash for a worthless document (their perception, not ours).

Through selective advertising you will minimize your cost and reach the people who are most likely to need your services. You should give a lot of thought to the strategy before you ever put it into action. Before spending a great deal on a large campaign, try your ideas with a test market. See what kind of response you get. Once you know what to expect you can more accurately

Another important consideration when designing advertising is to do it with quality. Always maintain a professional image with each advertising campaign you launch.

Your Office Location

You will need to decide where to locate the operations of your new business. A default mortgage purchasing business does not require high visibility on a busy street. As a result you can save a great deal of costs. Anywhere you can locate that has the simple necessities you will need is fine.

In many cases there is only one option. Lack of financing may necessitate that the business be out of your home. The vast majority of our students work out of their home. Still you may want to think about an office location for later when your business really gets going and you need more space.

You will need:

- A space to put a desk, a chair, a filing cabinet, and possibly little room for a visiting client if they come to see you (which is very unusual). This can be accomplished with as little as 100 square feet. You may want more room later but leave that until you can afford it.
- Additionally you will need a phone jack, and of course electric outlets.
- Your home situation may make it nearly impossible to do business there. If that is the case you should try to find an office. There are many ways economize with office space. When you are starting out, economizing may be a necessity. You may have a friend or relative who has extra space in an existing business. You may have access to a vacant apartment or addition to a friend's house. If there is a high vacancy rate in the commercial real estate sector, you may be able to negotiate a tremendous deal on some space with the first 1-2 months free. A local apartment complex may have several vacancies. You may be able to negotiate a deal for a small apartment to work from. Be creative and consider every option

Equipment

Here is an area that needs to be well thought out and planned. If you are like most start-up businesses you do not have unlimited funding. You will have to decide what equipment is most necessary and what you will have to do without, for a while anyway.

To start out, economize as much as possible. Once you become profitable you can turn some of the profits back into your company and acquire other items or upgrade the equipment  you have. Don't make the mistake of renting a plush office and furnishing it with stylish decor and state of the art equipment. Most start-up companies would not survive such a large negative cash flow in their beginning stages.

Equipment to consider acquiring may include the following:

- Computer
- Modem
- Various software programs
- Phones and additional phone lines
- Fax machine
- Printer
- Portable copy machine

(If you are completely computer illiterate I suggest that you sign up for a simple introductory course at the local community college, or spend a few hours with some of the self-paced tutoring programs you can install right on your computer. You can also visit your local computer store for a schedule of classes that are hosting by the computer store).

The Phone & Phone-Lines

In the beginning you can get away with using one phone line and sharing it between the computer, the phone and possibly a fax, but when you get going, this is going to become too complicated, if not impossible. (Not to mention rather inconvenient for your family if you happen to be monopolizing the only phone line in the house.)

You'll probably want to get a line dedicated to your computer and a separate one for your business phone. Additional lines into a home are not very expensive.

The FAX

For the at home office, look into getting a fax machine that has a phone and an answering machine in it. It should be able to differentiate between a phone call and a fax transmission automatically.

Another option is to have a fax board in your computer. This gives you a lot of flexibility, unless you receive a lot of faxes. This kind of program will generally run in the background waiting for a calls then when you receive a fax it will interrupt what you are doing and tell you that it's receiving. When the transmission is complete, it'll return control back to you.

Fax boards have the advantage of letting you store faxes on file and even manipulate the text and data in some programs. Pretty handy, and the print quality of the material is excellent compared to the often fuzzy look of a standard FAX. An example of this is available at eFax.com.

Printers

There are huge differences in the price, capabilities and quality of printers.

Laser

For top quality documents, letters, reports etc. you can't beat a laser printer. A laser printer actually sears the toner onto the paper. T he print quality is routinely 300 - 600 dpi. The price has dropped in the past few years and the number of options available is expanding all the time, like separate trays for feeding envelopes and various paper sizes. Some even duplex automatically. Lasers typically print from 4 - 12 pages per minute.

Ink Jet

These actually spray the ink on the paper, and can offer color options. They're slower thin lasers *(3* pages per minute) but they are less expensive.

What I have covered is just some of the basics of getting your own full-fledged business going with the least amount of hassle. You can do it. Don't let anyone else tell you otherwise. More people fail, not because they can't do the work, but because the support structure around them causes them to "believe" that they can't. I heard a phrase once "don't try …do". (Yoda from Star Wars). If you only try then you leave open the possibility that you will fail. If you just "do it" like the Nike commercial says you will be successful.

The above is not legal or accounting advice. Specific questions should be directed to your own professional advisors.

Form of Organization - Selection Chart		
Circumstances Surrounding Your Business	Recommended Form of Business Organization	Reasons for Recommended Form
One owner	Sole Proprietorship	Simplicity
Just starting-up	Sole Proprietorship	Requires that only a Schedule" C" be filed
Likely to generate an initial loss	Sole Proprietorship	Provides immediate low-cost start-up
Not certain you will stay with the business	Sole Proprietorship	Business loss can shelter personal income from other sources
Business becomes profitable	"S" Corporation	Can stop business without tax impact if no sales are made
More than one owner	"S" Corporation	You can take an appropriate wage plus tax favored distribution of profit
You provide a "professional service" (such as a doctor, lawyer, accountant)	"S" Corporation	Partnership form not recommended; keeps tax benefits of sole proprietorship plus other benefits of "S" Corporation
You anticipate selling the assets of your existing corporation	"S" Corporation	Avoids designation as a personal service corporation with its flat tax rate of 34%
Your business is profitable and you do <u>not need</u> or <u>want</u> to take dollars out of it	"C" Corporation	To avoid double taxation on sale of business assets (in effect if a "C" Corporation)
You already have a "C" Corporation, or are buying one that has a Net Operating Loss (NOL) carry-over	"C" Corporation	"C" Corporation tax rates stay lower longer (@ 15% up to $50,000) as compared to individual tax rates
Under <u>all</u> business circumstances	Partnership form not currently recommended	In this manner, you can offset future profits from this" C" Corporation with net operating loss carry-over

The above is not legal or accounting advice. Specific questions should be directed to your own professional advisors.

OK, Mike, But What If Something Goes Wrong?

I know I have spent some time talking about setting up your business, growing and even possibly hiring employees. I want to take a few minutes to tell you about something that happened to me that cost me over $3,000,000 and what I learned from that experience that I can pass on to you.

I am pretty sure I got your attention with the $3 million bucks. Well that was the financial loss but that was not everything.

This is also a story about getting in bed with the wrong people. Not that kind of bed; get your mind out of the gutter. My life lesson started way back around 2000. I decided to really ramp up my business and wanted to take it into the big leagues. I got started and I was creating a private placement fund to bring in investors who would pull together their resources; it was a small fund of $1 million dollars. The purpose of the fund was to start buying large pools of judgments and then force the payoff using everything I had learned about judgments and bad paper.

Now these were all sophisticated investors or accredited investors. They were pulling their funds together so that we could go out and invest that money and then hopefully get a good rate of return where the investors were getting a preferred rate of return back and they would also share in the profits of the Fund. I thought it would work out well, we would all make a lot of money and I would be on the way to the big time. Unfortunately, that's not what happened. What really happened and we'll kind of go into the story here, just so everybody understands what could happen, what could go wrong, and everything that could possibly go wrong does go wrong and in my case it really did go wrong.

We started to work the system and lo and behold right off the bat within a couple of months after we got started one of the investors decide that they want to pull their money out. The investor happened to be the largest investor who had put in $500,000 into the entire program, so he wanted out of the program and he said that he wanted his money out and I could either pay him his money or he would take it to court and tie me up in legal fees and everybody would end up losing their money while he's fighting to get his money back. It turns out he was a very litigious individual and loved to sue a lot of people. So I had to look at it from an investment standpoint what was better, give him the money back or fight him in court.

I was advised by the attorney while we felt that we would indeed win in court that we would end up spending all of the invested money trying to fight it in court and we would not end up doing what our original goal was, which was to invest our clients money and make above-market rate of return on their money. I had to approach each of the individual investors and ask permission to settle. They all signed off, saying it was okay for us to give the money back, because the alternative of fighting this individual in court was that nobody was making money. The problem with doing that, though, was that if we gave this individual back the $.5M that left us with a fund that only had half the amount of working capital that it needs to be successful. We wouldn't be able to have the proper staff, we wouldn't be able to make the right investments, so all of a sudden, now, right in the very beginning within the first couple of months, we immediately become underfunded . So I was left with the option of saying, how do I try to make this happen? How do I try to help my investors still make this goal so that everybody's happy? I certainly don't want my investors to lose money. Because at this point we had already invested most of that money to pay for a lot of different assets to try to get a return on our investment. We didn't have all that money; in fact, I had to take money out of my pocket to pay this $500k investor back. And I also had to try to keep the fund running to make sure that the investors wouldn't lose their investment. So I'm looking at not only their money, I'm looking at my money. I'm looking at my own personal reputation and I'm trying to make it all work, but we have problems. We continue on. We're trying to make it happen. We're starting to bring in some revenue. We're starting to get a return on our investments.

I found out that because we were short staffed and I was already managing several other businesses that I can't spend all the time to try to manage this Fund. I still need to bring somebody else in to help me. So I started looking for an individual to help me with that, and I'm not sure really who to go with and I find a couple of people. I hired some people who supposedly had experience in money call centers and upper level operations management and they were referred to be by some high level placement agencies. Guess what? Neither one of them worked. Within three months, we had them both fired , but yet now I'm still running into this time crunch since the fund is only designed to run for two years where I have to get it done; otherwise, I have to pay the investors out, or alternatively, I have to try to get an extension. So now the pressure's building. Folks, this is one area where the pressures can force you to make bad business decisions.

Here was my first big mistake and hopefully you'll learn from my mistake. I let pressure and fear, which ultimately stands for False Evidence Appearing Real, guide my decisions because I needed somebody to come in, quickly solve the situation, turn it around, because I was spending so much time trying to resolve this staffing and management issues of the Fund that my other businesses were starting to suffer, and now both companies were starting to suffer, because I can't manage them both properly. And I'm running against this time crunch. And we're running against a money crunch because we don't have to have money to run the fund properly. So I'm trying to handle it all.

Here's what happened. I was invited out to lunch with a friend of mine who says he wants me to meet somebody and have this conversation. So in this lunch meeting, he introduces me to this individual that he was referring as very high brow investment manager for MCI. In fact he was very high up in MCI and had glowing profit increases for the company. It sounded great. This would be the perfect person, and he thought he would be perfect to help me with my situation because I told him what was going on. I asked my friend, "do you know this guy"? He said yes, he vouched for him, he's a good guy and that it would work out great and that he could definitely help me. Here's where I made mistake number two. I didn't check the guy out. I should have done it. He gave me a basic resume. I looked at the resume, but I didn't actually follow up and call MCI where he said he was a VP at MCI. I didn't make that call. I pulled a credit report based on his information but that was all. I was thinking, who would ever make up that kind of a lie, that they're the VP of MCI? How stupid would that be? But really, how stupid was I, because I didn't check this out. You all can start to figure out that this is not going to work out for my benefit.

So I brought him into the organization and I showed him what we were doing and he was talking a good story of how he was going to make everything perfect and how he's got my back and will look out for me. By showing him what was going on I was also spending a lot of time pushing the fund along and guess what? We finally started to make some money. I turned it over to him to run the day-to-day operations and then within a few more months we stopped making money. All of a sudden, now, I actually have to take more money from my existing business and put it into the fund to keep it afloat while we try to make things happen and I can't figure out what's going on. So within the span of about 10 months, this is the time frame when I hired this individual, about 10 months later, all of a sudden I'm losing money left and right. Not only is the fund not making any money, and our return on investment is going down, we're not receiving any accounts receivable, no revenue is coming in, I'm losing money left and right and now I'm starting to panic. I start to dig into the books trying to figure out what's going on, and folks, listen to what happened. Learn from what I'm about to tell you. This is a nightmare situation that I hope never happens to you or anyone that you know.

I'm trying to figure out what's going on. So what I did is I started demanding copies of the books, and we were actually using QuickBooks at the time. I want to see copies of all the books. I want to see the check register. I want to find out what's going on from the beginning because I can't figure out where the money went or why we are no longer getting payments on the judgments we own. I can't make payments on my credit cards, I'm stressed, and we're supposed to have all this cash in the bank and it's not there. I am trying to figure out what's going on, I'm actually having a panic attack. I am talking to my accountant, who is handling the books for both the fund and my other companies, trying to figure out what is going on.

I set up a meeting with this individual. For our meeting I instructed Cranston (yes that is his name and I am not afraid to disclose it as you will soon see why) to bring me copies of the books, receipts etc. The morning of the meeting I am a little apprehensive so I call Cranston to make sure we are meeting this morning, yep, yep, yep, next thing you know I call him, hey, where are you? Oh, well he was in a fender bender, an auto accident, and now he is dealing with police reports and stuff like that, he said hey can I just hold off and he will meet me in just a little while. I wait a while and still no meeting. I called Cranston back and got delayed again. While I was waiting I was getting a very bad feeling in the back of my mind that something was going on. I realized have been blown off. So I immediately got in my car and drove down to the office and find out what is going on. I am tired of this.

So, I drive up to the office and some of the employees are actually loading computers and office furniture into some vans and they are packing stuff up. I am like, what's going on? They go, we don't know, we are just doing what we're told. I go into the office and there is nothing left in the office. Everything is gone except for a couple of chairs, there is one desk, all the phones, all the computers, everything is gone. Not only that, he took everything including my fish tank with my fish, took my Christmas tree. He took all the computers, all the software. He took everything, it was all gone. I am trying to figure out what is going on. There were a couple of people there and they were trying to say, oh, they didn't know what was going on, and when I first went in there and opened up the door, the door was locked. I am pounding on the door, let me in, and they let me in. What they were doing is they were getting off the phone with Cranston. They had called him to let him know I was there, and they thought I wasn't supposed to be there, so they didn't know what was going on. I am trying to figure out what's up and I am trying to get a hold of this guy. I am trying to get my stuff back.

I can't get a hold of Cranston so I call my lawyer and ask him what to do. My gut reaction is to find out where he took my stuff then go to his new office and just take my stuff back. My attorney advises me not to do that since I could be considered as trespassing. So I file a police complaint for theft. I also dug into the books in detail and guess what I found. I had $86,000 in forged checks, almost $300,000 in missing accounts receivable and over $600,000 in stolen equipment, furniture, software files etc. I even found documents from some of our collection attorneys where Cranston had told the attorneys and the employees that his company and my company had merged and they were no to send all accounts receivable to Cranston. That explained why the fund stopped making any money-Cranston was keeping it. I got written statements from the attorneys showing where the checks were deposited.

As it turns out the District Attorney's Office where I filed the complaint was doing and investigation of me based on information that was fed to them by Cranston and they refused to do anything about the thefts even when I showed them the evidence. Talk about adding insult to injury.

So now I am forced to sue Cranston in court to get my stuff back. Needless to say the Fund has completely shut down since I don't have any of the accounts or computers to keep things running. Fortunately I did have some old backups and immediately contacted all of our attorneys and investors to let them know what was going on. Some of the investors understood and others did not. Bottom line is I decided to negotiate payoff arrangements with the investors who were unhappy and continue to work with the ones who wanted me to sue Cranston and try and get our money back.

While I was negotiating with the other investors I was arrested by the district attorney's office and charged with theft of accounts receivable and securities fraud. I tried to show the DA's office where the money went (to Cranston's account not mine) but since Cranston was their star witness they wanted to pursue charges. They even threatened all of the investors in the Fund that if they did not go along with the charges they would not get any of their money back. Some investors sided with the DA and some sided with me.

Here is where we jump ahead 4 years of battling this out with the DA and never seeming to be able to get the case to go to trial. Each time it seemed like we were ready to go to trial the DA found a reason for delay. I even tried arbitration to settle the charges. I offered what I was originally trying to do before I got arrested which was to pay back all of the investors but this was refused by the DA's office.

It also turns out that Cranston was now wanted by the IRS and the FBI. It turns out he took US Bank for over $850,000. Apparently he was a habitual thief. In my research of Cranston I found out several pieces of interesting information. It turns out Cranston was not his real name. His name matched his social security number and when I pulled his credit report it all matched. The problem was that it was not his name or social security number. In fact it turns out he had four different names and socials and that he was previously shut down by the FTC for running and oil scam out of Texas and Florida. I passed all of this information on to the DA but it did no good.

Finally it looked like we were really going to go to trial. 2 days before the trial I decided to finally tell my children what was going on. It was one of the hardest conversations I have ever had. My kids asked me if daddy was going to jail and I told them that I did not think so but it was a possibility since it was a trial. They knew that Cranston sole all of my stuff and I could prove where the money went and they did not understand why I still had to go to court. I explained that sometimes you had to prove that you were innocent when people simply refuse to believe the facts and proof.

So guess, what? The day before the trial the DA postponed again. I was furious. More importantly I was done fighting. I could not take the emotional toll it was taking on me and my family and I told my attorney to settle the charges. I agreed to pay back all of the investors (I offered that several times since the beginning) and the DA's office would not release the case unless I agreed to plea to a felony. They said I had to take something. There would be no jail or anything like that but they had to have a plea. I ended up pleading to selling an ATM machine without a securities license. Go Figure. And, by the way, only in my county is an ATM considered a security.

So there I am. I paid off all of the investors and moved on with my life. At some point in your life to have to decide when to stop fighting city hall. They had a lot more money and a lot more time. All told I spent over $3,000,000, lost four years battling, the emotional stress on me, my wife and my kids. In the end I made the right decision to settle and most people when they hear the story agree with me that they would have settled as well. What would you have done?

I am so very thankful to my friends and my wife who believed in me and supported me though this stressful period in my life. In fact my relationship with my wife is better than it ever was. My wife and I now jokingly say we went through 20 years of couple's therapy in just four years because we had to really evaluate who we were as individuals, a couple, a husband and wife and a father and mother to our children. Our family is still together and we know that nothing can break us apart. I spend more time with my family than ever before and it is great. So I am thankful for the experience because I would not be who I am without having gone through this pain and suffering.

How could all of this been avoided? Well hindsight being what it is I should have checked out my employees better. Today I do background checks, credit reports and I have checks and balances so that no single employee has access to much information or control over the company. And never, ever let someone else control or supervise the money. If my name is on it I am in control. No one else, just me.

I share this story with you as a worst case scenario. I am still in business doing what I have always done. I have rebuilt my company and I am doing better than ever. The legal problems did not stop me they only slowed me down.

So what can you learn for my story? I have heard many stories from friends, clients and associates who tell me of how people that they trusted took advantage of them and stole lots of money leaving them holding the bag. I find it scary that there are lots of people who are willing to steal from you rather than work for a living. So be careful who you hire and who you let into your inner circle. As Ronald Regan our late President used to say "trust but verify". Ronald Regan wanted to believe all the agreements and promises that people have made to him, he would always trust that they would do what they said, but he would always verify. I have found, I can trust a lot of people, but you know what, I have learned that I need to verify because of hidden agendas. People can say all the things you want to hear, and it sounds really good and it looks good, on paper, but you need to keep in mind the hidden agenda.

You trust what people say, that's fine, but you verify. And if it doesn't match up, you know what; they don't deserve your trust. If they deserve your trust, verification won't hurt. They don't need to know that you're verifying.

I'm just trying to share with you all of the mistakes that I've made along the way and boy, oh boy, have I made a lot. The only thing I'm really guilty of is I'm guilty of making bad decisions.

I guess it's hard to put down on paper that I've made some bad decisions, but I own up to that. It's the best thing to do, because if you can learn from my bad decisions not to do the same things I did, then I've actually accomplished something and I turned a negative situation into a positive, not only for myself personally, but for you and the people that you know or the businesses that you're trying to grow. We trust but verify.

You still need to build a business and will eventually need employees. So keep your eyes open, watch your books and empower your employees to do what they do best.

How Mike Warren Can Help

In some of my three-day workshops people often come up to me and ask several of the same questions:

1. Doesn't it take money to make money?
2. Isn't investing risky?
3. How can you get such high returns without risk?
4. What if the stock market crashes?
5. What if we have a recession?

You can learn to take control of your financial future if you have the desire. If someone says, "you can't do that," it's not because you can't do it is because they cannot do it themselves. Remember, always consider your source of advice.

In today's society people want the greatest return with as little risk as possible. Some of the wealthiest people in the world got rich because they followed a simple financial plan. Saying to family members and to other investors that you invest in paper is not as glamorous as saying you own shares in Yahoo, Microsoft, General Motors or another big company. Knowing what kind of returns you are going to make over a specified time period is better than betting on the next IPO (Initial Public Offering.) You might be asking yourself "if this is such a great investment how come everyone is not doing it?" While this is an excellent question consider that most people reading this book did not know about this investment vehicle before they bought the book.

> **The best methods of investing**
> **may not be the most glamorous**

Some of the people who read this book would be interested in the ideas presented but will not have the financial resources to get started. Simply by finding judgment liens that Mike Warren purchases can provide you with the start-up capital you need to get going. We are receptive to anyone that can bring us judgment liens to buy. We pay a substantial finder's fee on each deal you bring us that we choose to buy.

Do you have a judgment that you would like money for and don't have the time to recover yourself? If so, please contact our office to see how we can help. Contact information is located in the back of this book.

CHAPTER NINE

GLOSSARY

The following glossary defines various terms that are used throughout this book. Use the glossary as a reference guide when reading through the special report to become familiar with the language of the judgment business.

Appraised Value: An opinion of the value of a property at a given time, based on facts regarding the location, improvements, etc., of the property and surroundings.

Bank Charge-off: A debt, such as credit cards, auto loans and personal loans that has been written off by the lending institution as uncollectable.

Default Judgment: Judgment entered in a lawsuit when a defendant has failed to enter a plea or otherwise defend himself.

Equity: The difference between the market value of the real property and any liens on the property.

Judgment: A legal document stating that a debt is owed from one party in a lawsuit to another party. The judgment will specify the amount of the award, attorney fees (if applicable), and the date on which interest on the unpaid balance begins.

Judgment Creditor: Any person or business which owns a judgment that has not been paid. Also called the plaintiff or creditor.

Judgment Debtor: Any person or business against whom a judgment has been obtained and who has not paid the amount of money owed to the judgment creditor. Also called the defendant or debtor.

Levy: When a law enforcement officer (Sheriff, Marshall) or registered process server acts under a Writ of Execution to obtain property or cash belonging to the judgment debtor for the purpose of satisfying the judgment.

Levying Officer: Usually the Sheriff or Marshall who is responsible for performing levies. This person will actually travel to the bank or employer to perform a garnishment.

Lien: A concrete legal assertion that you have a claim of a specific value against certain property.

Mechanics Lien: A claim created by a contractor or subcontractor when a builder or homeowner fails to make payment for work done in building or repairing a property. State laws govern these liens, but they can have priority over previously recorded liens. The holder of a mortgage or deed of trust cannot foreclose until mechanics liens have been satisfied.

Registered Process Server: An individual or someone who works for a company that makes a business out of serving legal documents.

Tax Lien: Lien for nonpayment of taxes.

Writ of Execution: A directive from the court to a levying officer within that court's jurisdiction. The Writ of Execution permits the levying officer to serve a levy on the judgment debtor's property based on instructions that judgment creditor has given to the levying officer.

Please visit our websites,

www.misuniversity.com

For information on:

- Educational Products

- Schedule Of Michael Warren's Judgment/
  Lien Three Day Workshops
- Public Speaking Schedule

Testimonials of Michael Warren's
Techniques and Programs

"My wife was looking for a career change and I want to support her endeavor. This business looks so appealing I'm going to ask to be her partner!"

Calvin K., California

"I learned enough to start my business succeed and become wealthy."

Don H., California

"Great Ideas. With these techniques, I will be making a substantial source of income."

Dan A., Illinois

"Very enlightening, increased my knowledge tremendously. More ways to create solutions to problems and money from it."

Barry S., Virginia

"I learned how to take advantage of skills I already have and with some experience get paid for something I really like to do."

Connie N., Ohio

FREE STUFF

Related Products

How To Make $13,571 a Month Stopping Foreclosure

This FREE CD will reveal how you can make a boatload of cold hard cash in today's troubled Real Estate market.

You'll discover many time-tested millionaire secrets straight from me, the nation's leading Foreclosure Real Estate expert and my 22 years of in-the-trenches real world experience.

This CD is valued at $24.95, but **I'm giving it to you for FREE!** But you have to hurry, because supplies are very limited.

http://www.misuniversity.com/lm1

Don't forget to ask:

"How can I get your educational programs for FREE?"

About The Author

Mike Warren's misuniversity.com is a website and company that teaches wealth building strategies primarily through real estate, especially in the areas of Judgments, Pre-foreclosures, defaulted mortgages and Short Sales. The company offers learning opportunities for real estate investors around the country through various on-site seminars, coaching programs, teleseminars, an interactive membership website, home study courses, and audio CD and DVD educational materials.

Mike Warren is a nationally known author, investor and instructor in the areas of collecting on real estate judgments and liens and making money with loan modifications, Deed in Lieu and short sales. Mike holds a double MBA, and is President of a diversified real estate consulting firm. TV and radio show hosts call Mike **America's Real Estate Assassin** because of his laser focus and his ability to get deals done.

Mike started in the business over 20 years ago and since then has bought and sold hundreds of properties that required little or none of his own money. Mike has developed the most comprehensive, systematic approach to buying and selling pre-foreclosures available today. Using his **Judgment & Lien Money Machine and**

Stopping Foreclosure Money Machine systems he has perfected the art of creating cash like no one else has. Michael teaches only what he has personally accomplished and has taught people all over America how to make fast, easy, and consistent profits using his innovative, creative, and proven techniques. Michael has appeared on television, has contributed articles in numerous real estate and related publications and speaks nationally and internationally on a regular basis to small and large groups.

BUY A SHARE OF THE FUTURE IN YOUR COMMUNITY

These certificates make great holiday, graduation and birthday gifts that can be personalized with the recipient's name. The cost of one S.H.A.R.E. or one square foot is $54.17. The personalized certificate is suitable for framing and will state the number of shares purchased and the amount of each share, as well as the recipient's name. The home that you participate in "building" will last for many years and will continue to grow in value.

Here is a sample SHARE certificate:

YES, I WOULD LIKE TO HELP!

I support the work that Habitat for Humanity does and I want to be part of the excitement! As a donor, I will receive periodic updates on your construction activities but, more importantly, I know my gift will help a family in our community realize the dream of homeownership. **I would like to SHARE in your efforts against substandard housing in my community!** *(Please print below)*

PLEASE SEND ME _____ SHARES at $54.17 EACH = $ $_____

In Honor Of: _____

Occasion: (Circle One)   HOLIDAY   BIRTHDAY   ANNIVERSARY

       OTHER: _____

Address of Recipient: _____

Gift From: _____ *Donor Address:* _____

Donor Email: _____

I AM ENCLOSING A CHECK FOR $ $_____ PAYABLE TO HABITAT FOR HUMANITY **OR** PLEASE CHARGE MY VISA OR MASTERCARD *(CIRCLE ONE)*

Card Number _____ Expiration Date: _____

Name as it appears on Credit Card _____ Charge Amount $ _____

Signature _____

Billing Address _____

Telephone # Day _____ Eve _____

PLEASE NOTE: Your contribution is tax-deductible to the fullest extent allowed by law.
Habitat for Humanity • P.O. Box 1443 • Newport News, VA 23601 • 757-596-5553
www.HelpHabitatforHumanity.org